relentless goodbye

relentless goodbye

Grief and Love
in the Shadow
of Dementia

Ginnie Horst Burkholder

 **Herald Press**

Harrisonburg, Virginia
Waterloo, Ontario

Library of Congress Cataloging-in-Publication Data
Burkholder, Ginnie Horst, 1944-
  Relentless goodbye : grief and love in the shadow of dementia /
Ginnie Horst Burkholder.
    p. cm.
  ISBN 978-0-8361-9616-0 (pbk. : alk. paper)   1. Lewy body
dementia—Patients--Family relationships. 2. Caregivers—Family
relationships. I. Title.
  RC521.B87 2012
  616.8'3—dc23
                                              2012007736

RELENTLESS GOODBYE
Copyright © 2012 by Herald Press, Harrisonburg,
Virginia 22802
  Released simultaneously in Canada by Herald Press,
Waterloo, Ontario N2L 6H7. All rights reserved.
Library of Congress Control Number: 2012007736
International Standard Book Number: 978-0-8361-9616-0
Printed in United States of America
Cover design by Reuben Graham, design by Joshua Byler

17 16 15 14 13 12   10 9 8 7 6 5 4 3 2 1

To order or request information, please call 1-800-245-7894 in the
U.S. or 1-800-631-6535 in Canada. Or visit www.heraldpress.com.

To Nelson and all like him who have fought to live with dignity in the grip of dementia.

To Eric Burkholder and Amy Regier and all those who have lived and loved in a relentless goodbye.

To Rich and Cora June who will never hear Papa Nelson's storytelling.

Contents

Foreword 11
Introduction 15

Year 10

The way it is 25
Is this Nelson? 29
Chronic sorrow 33
Humpty Dumpty kingdom 37
How we love 43
Good grief 47
Hurt and the holidays 51

Year 11

Change is the one constant 57
Living and managing life with LBD 61
On the long road to acceptance 65
Word salad 71
Respite and the re-entry blues 77
Banish the Judge 81
Visiting the memories 85
Living with the dissonance dragon 89
Tug of war 93

Giving thanks. 97
A caregiver's Christmas list 101

Year 12

My new year 107
Struggle and hope. 111
A longing and a gift. 115
The communication conundrum 119
Lost power 123
Before and after. 127
What can he do today? 131
Kaleidoscope 135

Year 13

I have survived 141
Sometimes it matters 147
Bridging the gap 153
What can I do? 159
Another go at freedom 163
It is time 167
A caregiver's prayer. 173
Three times a lady 177
No bed in long-term care 181

Year 14

Waiting. 189
Longing to be known. 193
Long-term care but still a caregiver. 197
Finding Nelson 201
How many times can you say goodbye? 205
The hardest thing. 209

Maybe this is mercy 213
How are you doing? 217
Taking care of me. 221
Voices. 225

Year 15

Happy you, sad me. 231
Promises, promises 235
Give feelings a voice 241
A cleaner grief 247
No words for his grief 253
Going forward 259

Afterword .265
Acknowledgments 267
About the author 271

Foreword

Throughout my years as a grief counselor, educator, and author, I have come more and more to value what I call "the telling of the story." When you experience loss, it is human nature to want to tell what happened. Usually this takes the form of talking to someone else, preferably someone with good listening ears. The story often starts with a brief summary of "the way things used to be," followed by a detailed retelling of what transpired as the loss unfolded.

If you are telling your story, it's a sign that you're doing your work of mourning. Whether you're conscious of this fact or not, you tell yourself the story and you tell others the story in an effort to integrate it into your life. What has happened to you—the decline and eventual death of someone you love—is so hard to fathom that your mind compels you to revisit it and revisit it and revisit it until you've truly acknowledged it and embraced its presence.

Telling the story helps bring your head and your heart together. It is also a way of giving voice to your grief, of taking the grief that is inside of you and expressing it outside of you. This is *mourning*—expressing your thoughts and feelings of grief. And embracing the need to mourn is the path that leads to eventual healing.

In this tender yet never cloying memoir, Ginnie Horst Burkholder tells the story of her long journey through grief as she cared for her precious husband, Nelson, even as she was losing him to dementia day by day.

When someone has it in them to tell their story in the form of a book, their story can help others. Ginnie's book may be read by thousands of people, all of whom are seeking affirmation and articulation of their own personal thoughts and feelings. In writing well and in telling her story in poignant scenes, Ginnie allows us intimate glimpses into her life that in turn give us perspective on our own.

My mother suffered from Alzheimer's and eventually required the care of a specialized assisted living facility. Even though I do not pretend to fully understand Ginnie's years caring for and losing Nelson, I know something of the devastating experience of losing someone twice—once to dementia and later to death. Yes, when someone we love has dementia, we grieve and we grieve and we grieve. We grieve the diagnosis, we grieve the many big and little losses along the way, and one day we grieve the death.

As anyone who has ever been a caregiver can attest, love is a verb. To truly love someone means to act on that person's behalf in compassionate, selfless, and kind ways. No one understands the maxim "love is a verb" better than caregivers to those with dementia, like Ginnie. It's important, then, to keep in mind that love and grief are two sides of the same coin and that grief, too, requires action.

The path to healing requires that we *mourn*, that we express our grief outside of ourselves. Mourning is grief in action. Mourning is the verb form of grief. Ginnie mourned, in part, by writing this book. How will you express *your* grief? How will *your* grief become a verb?

In my own book *Healing Your Grieving Heart When Someone You Care About Has Alzheimer's*, I claim that love lives on. Love is not a function of the brain and cannot be eliminated by brain disease. Faulty chemicals and circuits in the brain cannot affect love. Love is in our hearts and in our souls. Love endures.

This lovely book helps us hold that precious truth above all others.

—Alan D. Wolfelt, PhD
director of the Center for
Loss and Life Transition
www.centerforloss.com
March 2012

Introduction

In 1991 a small group from our church leadership team sat around a table to take a personality test, just "for fun." It was obvious that Nelson needed more help in following the directions than seemed warranted. I blamed it on poor sleep.

During the previous decade, sleep disturbances had gradually become more frequent and troublesome. Nelson would dream he was in danger and lash out or even bolt from the bed and leave dents or holes in the wall. I began to sleep with my back to him, fearful for my safety.

In December of 1992 when the sleep episodes became intolerable, we saw a sleep specialist. Nelson was diagnosed with REM behavior disorder. They told us that the normal mechanism that keeps us from acting out our dreams was not working and prescribed Klonipin, making him zombie-like.

What was happening? Nelson was a physically active and fun-loving man in his forties.

We had built a good life together. Nelson and I spent the first six years of our marriage in Chicago doing voluntary service and then working our way

Nelson creating a tale for daughter Amy in our back yard in Canton, Ohio, 1982

through college at the University of Illinois Chicago Circle campus. After graduation Nelson was offered a teaching job in Canton, Ohio, close to my family. We quickly adopted First Mennonite Church as our second family. Our two children, Eric and Amy, were born in Canton. Over the next fourteen years, we were absorbed in our children, church, extended family, and friends.

Nelson and I had both grown up on farms and I yearned for a garden. In 1986, when Eric was thirteen and Amy seven, we moved to a tiny, run-down, two-story, one-hundred-year-old house on two acres. Nelson enjoyed renovations and I loved working in the yard and garden. We reveled in the spaciousness even though we had taken on a huge project both indoors and out. We worked hard and then played hard, hosting hot dog roasts and volleyball games with family or friends.

Eric taught us to play Frisbee football and we would extend an open invitation to our small church family for Sunday afternoon games. I could keep up pretty well with the rest of the mostly younger players even though I was into my forties. Nelson was

Nelson relaxing with son Eric on our front porch swing, Canton, Ohio, 1982

strapping strong. He could carry two bundles of shingles up a ladder to the second-story roof as if it were nothing, so a little Frisbee football was no sweat.

But now something was wrong.

We stumbled through the next few years with different doctors and diagnoses and medications that never seemed to resolve the problems. With each diagnosis we would wait to see how the medications would work, and then when we didn't see satisfactory results, the doctor would try something else.

We saw a neurologist who diagnosed depression and prescribed Zoloft and visits to a therapist. Then this same neurologist added a diagnosis of attention deficit disorder and prescribed Dexedrine. More time elapsed until I took Nelson to a neuropsychologist who administered extensive psychological tests. She told us, "He has brain damage." The doctor asked if he had fallen. Since he hadn't, she had no explanation. For the sleep disorder, she suggested having the TV on and eating turkey before bedtime. Five hundred dollars and I felt we were getting nowhere.

By the fall of 1995, Nelson's symptoms were troubling enough that he had to quit teaching fifth and sixth grades. We took Eric to college in Goshen, Indiana. Amy was now in high school. I was working and juggling doctor visits while trying to understand and adjust to new manifestations of the disease. At the same time, a health problem that had plagued my own adult life now became more pronounced: chemical sensitivities.

We began making many visits to the Cleveland Clinic where Dr. Eric Geller's compassion and determination endeared him to me immediately. I felt we finally might get some help. "There's a long list of things it could be. We will go through the list until we find out what it is." An x-ray showed that Nelson had something called sarcoidosis. We thought we had our answer. After nearly a year with puffy cheeks from taking Prednisone and enduring endless testing, Nelson's symptoms still could not be explained. Dr. Geller did not believe it was Alzheimer's and he wanted us to see a doctor he had studied under at Northwestern Medical Faculty Foundation in Chicago.

It was from that visit to Chicago in December of 1996 that Nelson, at age fifty-one, was finally given an accurate diagnosis of Lewy body dementia, also called dementia with Lewy body disease or DLBD. (In this book I will use LBD as the acronym.)

Nelson with me and son Eric, Christmas 2011

Since then I've looked back and realized how in my confusion, disbelief, anger, fear, and frustration I was often not there emotionally for our children. Amy's high school years were a blur of medical distractions, and at times she became mother to Mom in order to ease things for me. I remember looking into her face one difficult evening and seeing the sadness that I knew was on my own. The opportunities for normal give and take in the growing relationships with father and spouse were gradually disappearing. We had to change and compromise expectations. For Eric it was the loss of opportunities to build a relationship with his most significant role model. Beautiful people that they are, our kids have lived forgiveness and have admonished us not to live in regrets.

At the time of diagnosis, there was very little information available about LBD, but after all we had been through, knowing what it was seemed like relief

Nelson with daughter Amy and grandaughter Cora, in his room at Canterbury Villa of Alliance, Ohio, Thanksgiving 2011

enough. The relief was short-lived, however. Lewy body has dementia symptoms that resemble Alzheimer's as well as kinetic symptoms that resemble Parkinson's. One of the symptoms somewhat unique to LBD is fluctuating cognition—an aspect of the disease that keeps caregivers on an emotional rollercoaster. It also makes it easy to explain away initial symptoms: "It could happen to anybody." Other typical symptoms listed by the Lewy Body Dementia Association are hallucinations, transient and unexplained unresponsiveness, delusions, illusions, visual impairment, sleep disturbances such as are seen in REM behavior disorder, and autonomic dysfunction. Some experts now say that LBD is the second leading cause of dementia, but that it is often misdiagnosed as Alzheimer's.

The literature available at diagnosis said that average life expectancy was seven years but that it could be as long as twenty. I couldn't wrap my mind around the twenty-year possibility, which we are now well on our way to achieving. I focused then on getting through those seven years of unknowns and doing what I had to do, even though they looked daunting.

Even with a diagnosis there was no hope for real improvement. Accepting the implications of the diagnosis was a huge hurdle for me, and I needed help from many sources. Friends and mentors helped me to name and face my fears. I focused on healing some of the emotional baggage I had brought with me to this stage of my life, baggage that fed the terror I felt about losing my capable, vivacious partner. I came back to journaling. I spent time with a therapist. I prayed and was part of an emotional healing group for many years. I needed all of these to help me process what was happening to my world, which seemed to be wobbling right off its axis.

This book didn't start out to be a book. My writing was simply my tool for processing the changes that were mandated by LBD and the emotions they triggered as dreams and expectations scattered and fell away.

Writing was my voice for truth as I experienced it on any given day. I needed to give voice to the whole story—to the reiterated loss, ongoing grief, underlying pain, and the constant struggle in and out of acceptance. I also needed to combat the isolation that creeps into the life of a caregiver. I began to post my writing on the Lewy Body Dementia Association website[1] and received numerous responses from other caregivers over the years. Some of these are included in this book.[2]

The stories and reflections in this book repeat the themes of loss, grief, and the struggle for acceptance. That is what a relentless goodbye is. It means grieving the loss of today and coming to terms with a different expectation of your spouse. Then, just when you've figured out how to cope, you start all over because now there is something new falling away in this snail-paced, growing-down goodbye.

I have learned so much and grown in ways I value and couldn't have imagined. Still, this journey is a hard teacher. I've heard people say about difficult experiences that they wouldn't change a thing. Maybe someday I will say that. I just know that I'm not there yet.

---

1. www.lbda.org
2. Names with quotation marks are pseudonyms to protect privacy.

YEAR 10

Blessed are those who mourn.
—Matthew 5:4 NIV

People say I am strong.

Lord, I want to be weak.

I want to give up and let someone else take over.

I want to cry out my grief and let someone else worry about what
to do and how to do it, worry about who is going to take care of
everything, worry about what will happen in the future.

I am not strong.

I only do what I have to do.

I take in my loss, and his loss, and our children's loss,

and grieve it over and over until

I come to some sort of ability

to let go of the Nelson of the past

and then cope with the present.

Then I start all over again because by now he is able to do

less than he was before,

is present less than he was before,

is gone farther from us than he was before,

and now needs me more than ever before.

—GHB

The way it is

June

I'm wide awake. It's the middle of the night, when the world caves into one little room and the only thing you know for sure is that the darkness has exposed all your fears. I have had him up to the bathroom to avoid the more frequent accidents due to incontinence, but back in bed, I feel anxious.

I don't want to think about when I can't manage. Nelson can hardly get himself up. I tug and pull on arms and legs. Getting him back into bed is no easier. He's too high, with his head against the headboard and can't reposition. Or he is too low, with feet hanging out and over the edge. Or he lies kitty-corner. Finally, I ask if he's comfortable. As always, he says yes.

So I'm awake at 2:30 a.m. Isn't it supposed to get easier at some point? Aren't you supposed to just be able to finally say this is the way it is, no more pining for what can't be? When does that time come? When do I get to feel light and free again? When do I get to know that I can relax and the clothes will not get wet, or the water will not be left filling the sink, or the food will not end up on the floor? When do I get to breathe deeply without dipping into the sadness that makes its home in the pit of my stomach?

Nelson used to call me "babe." We were young then, and our lives were a kaleidoscope of normalcy. He would toss me a wink on a whim or make a joke—something I bristled at when I was serious. He had boundless energy and was never sick. I had bouts of respiratory reactions to environmental triggers and allergies. "I get so tired of your being sick," Nelson said to me one day when I was down. During his twenty-one-year teaching career, he taught fifth and sixth graders and collected sick days like trophies.

We were like the morning glory and the evening primrose—he his best in the morning, I more lively at night. In our earliest years, I would wake up in the morning to find him sitting in our rocking chair nursing (his word) a cup of steaming coffee and studying for one of his college courses. I would climb onto his lap and melt into my sleepiness for a few quiet moments together.

We would leave our third-floor walk-up apartment in Chicago for college classes; or in the summer, he would head to his job driving a Chicago city bus or taxi. He would come home with stories of inebriated or colorful riders. Nelson entertained audiences for years to come, mimicking the drunk that was unable to pronounce his own street. Or he would tell about the gun a rider brandished or the mattress in the middle of the street that he straddled with his taxi cab. He would laugh until he couldn't talk as he remembered dragging the mattress along and then watching it tumble down the street behind him. Safe in our bed at night, I would stretch my toes to touch him as I fell asleep and then awake blanketed in the comfort of knowing he was nearby.

I've heard people say, "You have your memories," as if they are something to sustain you. But when I remember life before Lewy body dementia (LBD), the ache and the longing for what was and can never be again grow into a consuming sadness. It seems best not to remember the husband of the past. I must let that Nelson go.

We have just spent another night of trying to correct my husband's kitty-cornered sleeping pose, with his feet hanging off the side, and no place in the bed for me. Now he's experiencing unpredictable angry outbursts over trivial things, and I'm at a loss how to deal with the accusations, threats, and name-calling. Things just keep getting sadder.
—"Olivia"

It amazes me that even in the medical field I get blank stares when I tell them what he has.
—"Lynette"

Our neurologist has been saying all along that my husband doesn't have LBD. On our last visit he gave my husband a memory test and was surprised at how poorly he did. I showed him the LBD brochure with the symptoms listed. My husband has all but one. The doctor finally said I could call it LBD if I wanted to.

—"Ruby"

Think of a time when good memories sustained you. Think of a time when good memories reminded you of loss. What do you think the memories would do for you as a caregiver?

Is this Nelson?

July

When we eat out I take along all the equipment we need to manage the tremors and the obstacle they are to eating: antibacterial wipes, a tablespoon, paper towels, and a tea towel discreetly placed in his lap. We don't hesitate to ask the waitress for more napkins. Sometimes he asks for help when he needs it. Sometimes I give him help when he thinks he doesn't. It's all part of eating out.

The sizzling summer day has cooled, and after the meal the weather invites us to an evening outdoors. We decide to play a game of miniature golf. Nelson starts out okay, but soon I see he is tiring, needing more and more prompts. When I ask if he wants to take his turn, he signals that he doesn't. This is not my Nelson. This is someone I do not know.

Who is this man? The Nelson I know loves to play. He is the teacher who spends noon hours at the school fair playing ball with the students and volunteering for the dunking machine. "Put in a dollar! Make the teacher holler!" he calls. When he comes out laughing, dripping wet and shivering, our daughter, Amy, asks where he comes up with these things, and he says only, "My back pocket, I guess." He has little time to wonder about that. The next fair adventure is calling his name.

The Nelson I know is the father who celebrates the downpour at the end of a long drought by grabbing a five-gallon bucket and heading for the overflowing downspout. No one is safe but me, since I have the camera. He darts after each of the children who have their own buckets. He brings Kits, the family cat, into the fray. The claws are out, but that doesn't stop Nelson from holding a gleeful baptism under the downspout.

He is the uncle who fills balloons with water at family reunions and then at just the right moment throws the first balloon at some distracted nephew who is big enough to get him back good.

He is the husband who entices me into games I have never played and adventures I would not choose alone.

But now he needs a bench. We take turns sitting with him while we play a few more holes. His head droops lower and lower. A player in a Harley-Davidson tee shirt strolls by: "Is he okay?" I nod, but there are lingering concerned glances from the biker. I am always touched when people show concern in even the smallest way.

I ask if he wants to try to play again. "I want to go home," he says. This is unheard of. This can't be

Nelson. You would think that ten years into an LBD diagnosis nothing would surprise me. But a little vacillation into normalcy often lures me into expecting to see more of the Nelson I once took for granted. He can be his old self for five minutes or two hours or even a day. When that happens, I relax my guard and begin to believe he is back. Then suddenly, as now, I come face to face with a stranger and the sharp ache of loss.

I walk alone to the distant parking lot and then drive around to pick him up where he waits with the others.

The next day we break our midmorning date to walk to a neighborhood yard sale with a friend; Nelson needs to sleep a little longer. He and I go later when he is more rested. Still, he stays in the car most of the time, so we don't stay long.

My disappointment with the afternoon grows when at home he has a burst of energy and begins to rake the yard. Now, I wonder, why now? I get out the hedge trimmers and begin to cut away at the overgrown hedge as if it were my dissatisfaction. It is a long hedge, but the task is nothing compared to the emotional work of living with a husband who is both with me and lost to me.

I call him dude when he's not himself. That's my way of reminding me, he's not himself.
—Linda Cason

He was brilliant, he was funny, he was a man who could do anything. He built a guest house from the bottom up and repaired anything that needed fixing. Now he's broken and no one can fix that.

—"Frances"

My sixty-six-year-old mother was diagnosed today with LBD after eleven months of chasing a diagnosis. I am experiencing a weird mixture of relief and grief. Relief that we finally know and grief that the woman who raised me is slipping away, and there's nothing I can do about it.

—Diana Blackstone-Helt

Have you ever watched someone lose characteristics that once made them unique and special to you? If so, how did you react? If that person were your spouse, how would the change affect you? How would it be different if it were your parent? Your child?

Chronic sorrow

August

I'm reading a book by Susan Roos called *Chronic Sorrow*. The title stands out like a beacon. Roos has opened my heart and dissected its dull ache into knowable little pieces. I'm reminded that I'm not weird or weak or too needy. I'm responding as people do when they are faced with a loss that unfolds new consequences day after day until years have stacked up.

She tells me the disconnect I feel with "normal" people is not unusual. I can't relate to their way of ordering the world. They can't relate to mine. I don't mark time by the same events as they do: retirement treats, pursuing common interests beyond what early marriage allowed, assisting or following adult children. If I mark time at all, I mark it by the losses and crises that litter the path of a caregiver.

Roos sees what most people can't—that the more I attempt to make life normal for Nelson, the more abnormal life becomes for me. Yes, he can still enjoy the paintbrush in his hand, the sense of accomplishment, the satisfaction of doing a job at which he was once so adept. But someone needs to get in the car and go for the paint; make sure the brush is still usable; map out and monitor the steps of scraping, priming, painting; note what has been overlooked as he paints; and clean up afterward. While others look at him and say he is doing so well, Roos sees the scramble it creates for me the caregiver.

There's a double bind in chronic sorrow. I want to be with other couples, but when I am, I see so many should-have-beens that trigger feelings of loss. I can avoid those triggers by isolating myself, but then the loneliness increases. I've learned to live in both places, weighing in the moment which place is least discomforting: being with others and facing the triggers, or staying away and facing the loneliness.

Roos tells me to separate the disease from the man. I recognized this distinction soon after diagnosis. I knew I needed to take out my anger on the disease and not on Nelson. It sounds simple, but at times it seems impossible. When my life repeatedly has to bend and mold to his needs, or when I just want the comfort of someone else's competency to fall back on, he and the disease meld into one.

Our family physician says he sometimes forgets that behind Nelson's flat facial expression there is often a smile. How do you know a person if not by their expressions and their behaviors? How do you know a person if not by how they respond and what they present? It seems I'm being asked to base my knowing him on memories and gritty should-have-beens.

Fantasies, Roos tells me, have a lot to do with how we cope. My fantasy has always been about mutual companionship, comfort, and support. If my fantasy had been about taking care of someone, pouring out myself for someone else's need, it would have been an easier adjustment. But whose fantasy is only about giving? Dismantling a fantasy is exhausting.

I grew up in a family of eight children. I was the oldest of the second four children and had some responsibility for younger siblings at the same time that I needed something from my parents that they were not equipped to give me. Life with Nelson brought a comfort and support that I'd not experienced before. Having it taken from me throws me back into the feelings of a child adrift in the world with responsibilities that seem too big for me.

Roos talks about families who disintegrate initially and then begin to pull together. I didn't know how to cope with my own uncertainties, losses, and fears. Our two children, one in high school, one in college, were also experiencing loss but I couldn't help myself, let alone them. They were losing not only their father but their mother. Now we're learning as we go how to be family.

Finally, Roos talks about faith. My faith in God feels blunted, as if I can't quite hold on to it. But neither can I let it go. Diminished faith is protection, she tells me, from further feelings and perceptions of betrayal and disappointment. For now some part of me lies quietly, deep inside a place of knowing that ultimately God is good. The rest of me is tentatively waiting for the storm to pass to see if God will appear beside me. It's hard to see in the thick of the storm and it's hard to hear my name.

Absolutely nothing would get me to read about my current incarceration. Every free moment I'm running away from it. Probably not the healthiest response, but my fantasies were never to be a caregiver. That's the masochistic type, no?

—"Liz"

I am fifty-one years old and have been caring for my fifty-four-year-old husband for seven years. He has lost thirty pounds, is in a diaper, and cannot walk or feed himself. I placed him in a nursing home and my heart is burning with pain. I feel as though I have failed him.

—"Connie"

How well do you think you would do at bending and molding your life to the needs of a person with dementia? If you have ever "dismantled a fantasy," what was it like? What fantasy would you have to dismantle if your spouse developed dementia? Or your parent?

Humpty Dumpty kingdom

September

I have been halfheartedly looking at houses for sale, believing that someday I will make the change that seems mandated by this disease. I saw one that had a picket fence that I liked. But the yard was overgrown and full of thistles. It took me back to when we bought these two acres, all overgrown and having so much potential. But I have done potential and potential means lots of work, and I alert myself to the twenty years of wear and tear to which my body has succumbed since then. Now I need order and an invitation to comfort.

Twenty years ago we were full of energy. We could work all day and play in the evening. On summer days or weekends when Nelson wasn't teaching, he tore into the major overhaul of a one-hundred-year-old farmhouse and doubled its size from two to four bedrooms while I planted grass seed. I dragged an old bed spring across the dirt and stones to level the soil. We were healthy and in love with God's creation. We loved our part in bringing order and creative energy to these two acres.

In the evening after a day of painting the ancient small barn, Nelson would want to walk around what he called "our kingdom." We would note that the river willow we had planted was still alive and that the ash tree was getting big. We would stop to pleasure at the flashing feathers of bluebirds occupying the boxes Nelson had placed along the garden. We would check on each growing thing and breathe deeply of the air that was oxygenated by the tall wild cherry trees that bordered our property on the west.

We didn't know it then, but we had less than ten years to create this kingdom before we would find ourselves like Humpty Dumpty at the bottom of our kingdom wall in a thousand pieces.

Over the years, we added blueberry bushes and dogwood trees that we dragged in sleds from the woods, redbuds, butterfly bushes, flowers given by friends, and chocolate peppermint tea from a nursery. We ate the tea leaves chopped up fine and sprinkled over vanilla ice cream. Our daughter, Amy, and I thought it exquisite. Nelson wasn't so sure.

We adopted a cat we named Kits that followed Nelson or our son, Eric, up the ladder when they painted or trailed along for strolls in the woods. Later, a puppy we named Doogie Bowser MD (for mad dog) joined us. A hopeful student had given him to an even more hopeful Nelson. Everyone except the cat and I welcomed the floppy-eared mutt.

Today the children are grown and gone to other states. The dog and the cat are both just a memory. I've started to wonder if I will ever be able to let go of this Eden we have created. I feel it happening ever so slowly, matching pace, perhaps, with the disease. I've mowed over some flower beds. Tendonitis, hurting joints, reflux, and sometimes discouragement or despair have curbed my interest and ability to take care of them as the grass invades.

At the same time, Nelson's ability to help maintain our kingdom has diminished. Some days he can help. The next day he can't. With his brain scrambled by LBD, I begin to think of our kingdom as the Humpty Dumpty kingdom where all the king's horses and all the king's men can't put Humpty together again.

Now I must be open to change. I see the beginning of letting go in the shrinking garden, in the grapevines not pruned, the empty canning jars, the quiet house, and the diminished pleasure in potential. It is beautiful here, but it is lonely.

I tell myself that when it is time I will let go. There are other kingdoms. I have prayed for an internal one in an often repeated litany, "Thy kingdom come in me, in Nelson." I list family and friends as well. In my best moments, I can believe the kingdom is coming no matter what happens to us or our Humpty Dumpty kingdom. In my worst moments, this prayer somehow helps me let God off the hook for all the suffering I do not understand.

This week I transplanted a sapling redbud tree that had sprung up too close to the house. I found a place for it down over the hill where it will be in full view of our large kitchen window. In a few years when it blooms with its delicate pink flowers and burgundy leaves, it will be a smashing spring spectacle. I would so like to see it then.

Thy kingdom come . . .

Stories she was telling her family members were outrageous, but they continued to believe her.

—"Lola"

Ed doesn't talk much, and I often feel very lonely. I was raised by a father who "took care of me" and then I married a man who did the same—now I'm learning to prepare income tax reports, keep up with car maintenance, pay bills, etc. Sometimes I feel widowed already.

—Jane Griffith

It was a long trail down, both of us grieving at first over the death of our plans for retirement. When he began to get dementia, there was much less grieving together. And then when he died, I thought I had grieved enough, so I was astonished to find myself buried in grief. Now, after almost two years, I am beginning to find that woman of twenty years ago, but she is very different—white haired, wrinkled arms, low energy. But at least the future is mine.

—Carolyn Vanderslice

Dementia brings loss and forces change. What changes have been forced on you by circumstances? What were the circumstances? How did you respond? How do you think you would handle the forced change brought on by dementia of a spouse? A parent? A sibling?

How we love

___

October

Since this is the month of our anniversary, I have been thinking about weddings. As I reminisce I read again what I wrote in 2004, eight years into the Lewy body diagnosis. We had just attended a niece's wedding. By this time the support systems were in place, and we had dealt with many of the logistics of living with this disease, but I continued to struggle with acceptance.

Something tight and sad reaches inside and wraps itself around me at weddings. It's the fairytale that should have been, the bright, promising future that could have been, the hope and the promise that went away. A pastor's story about the changes in life that took a couple back to the wedding vows with a different perspective each year only sharpened my sadness. I am acutely aware that for Nelson, that potential is slipping away with each year of LBD.

How do you embrace love that is so incredibly needy? How do you let go of wanting to receive just a little normalcy? I decide I hate weddings. While others might be seeing hope and anticipating the future, I am seeing disappointment and burying the future. My sister sees my struggle during the ceremony and reaches past Nelson to touch my arm; her comforting gesture makes the tears harder to control. I sit there biting down on the sadness, my eyes wet, and my nose running. The couple says their vows, and Nelson reaches his hand toward me, prodding. I turn questioning eyes, and he pulls my hand into his and holds it. He loves me so much and yet can't be what I want or give what I need, which, at the moment, is tissues and comfort. When will I ever learn to carry tissues to weddings and funerals?

When they introduce the bride and groom and then tell them to kiss, Nelson turns toward me. I think he has a question, and I lean close to him. He kisses me on the cheek. I am deeply touched and feel love and lost to love.

What is it? I am not sure. I know what commitment is. We have that. But love? It seems like this impossible dream that teases me, and I forever believe it is possible. But just when I think maybe I have it, it seems to evaporate because love is supposed to be a two-way giving, a two-way sharing, a two-way managing, a two-way effort, and it all feels so one-way; I do not yet know how to love when so many supposed-to-bes have gone away with no hope of returning, and I am left holding all the responsibility with absolutely no room for letting Nelson cover my back, but always and forever, I need to cover his.

This week we celebrated forty years of marriage. Our anniversary open house was a great time. There were glitches, like the coffee on the shirt at the last minute. What shirt now? Can't be this one, or we have to change pants, too, in order to match. This isn't as nice, but it will have to do. It doesn't matter as much as it once would have. We no longer have the energy to fight such things. They are only speed bumps.

Nelson wanted to buy a card for me. I needed to get him one too, so we went to the drugstore. Then, helping him find an appropriate card to give me, I wondered why on earth I hadn't brought along one of the family, sitting back at the house, to cover this. I forgave us both—him for having the disease, myself for not thinking ahead. Later, we exchanged the cards in a private moment and then were swept up in the momentum of the open house. There were pictures. There were goodies. We greeted, we mingled, we remembered, and we laughed.

Maybe love is not defined by what the other can give to you, but by who they allow you to be. I allow for his disease, his forgetfulness, and even his denial. He allows for my bungling, emotional, sometimes impatient caregiving. For now this is how we love.

*One of the first of many goodbyes was to sex!
Caresses disappeared next, and cuddles are on the
way out too. I miss the closeness of intimacy.*

—Juliet Way

*It is so painful that memories of happier and
healthier times have faded, because I am face-to-face
each day with the reality of what is happening to a
wonderful human being. I keep pictures and videos
available, and I rerun the past in my mind, but it
often isn't enough.*

—Linda Koutoufas

How do you see yourself coping with a relationship
that has "one-way giving"? What is love to you?
Have you ever sustained a relationship with someone
who has had progressive dementia? If yes, how did
you sustain your love?

Good grief

November

I'm told that if I grieve and mourn well, healing and acceptance will come. Being the spouse of someone who has dementia requires grieving. Expect me to grieve.

In *The Year of Magical Thinking* Joan Didion writes about the subtle changes in the body that accompany grieving. A lower body temperature is one. No wonder I am always cold. Disturbed cognition is another. Indeed, for ten years I have lived in a body where the physiological changes that accompany grief fog my own cognition. Concentration more often eludes me. Enthusiasm and energy for life are harder to come by.

"Live the dying process for ten years," I say in an imaginary conversation with no one in particular. "Live with this kind of loss and grief, and see what it does to your cognitive function." I feel validated, justified for the anger that creeps back into my awareness at intervals.

No, I do not remember that so-and-so was at that event. Don't ask me to remember the things that serve no purpose except to prove that my brain is fogged by this cycling in and out of grief, shock, denial, anger, and magical thinking.

Acceptance is so elusive. How can it not be? You are strung in some in-between place where there is neither death nor moving on. Some say you choose your emotions. How do you watch the cognitive functions of your husband disappear for ten years and choose to be okay with that? How? You don't. Still, parts of you have to move on toward acceptance. But another part stays behind in that in-between grieving place where you try to live out your commitment to "till death do us part."

A couple of weeks ago, as we were about to leave church, someone helped me put on my coat. "I saw someone help Nelson with his," she said. "I will help you with yours." I told her that it feels good to be pampered. That was the word I used: *pampered*. "You don't get much of that do you?" she said.

Sometimes words lay open a truth that you are trying hard not to notice. I felt my lips go into a hard line, as if that could silence the truth. It didn't, of course. It only held back the toxin-removing tears and delayed the healing that comes with emotional truthfulness. It seems "good grief" is not just an expression; it is the necessary journey of a caregiver.

I find myself in and out of cognition myself. Marv will say, "Aha! Maybe I need to send you to my doctor." But there is so much on my mind. Three more years before I can retire. Do we have enough medical coverage? Can he really accept that I am doing the checkbook now? How long will it be before he is so confused again? I have had some recurring chest pain for the past few months. I have just chalked all of this up to stress.

—Loretta Cortelyou

I just seem out of it most of the time. Can't seem to get a grip on things and feel things are swirling out of control. Been making some bad decisions and not reacting normally to things. Finally, made a call to arrange for some help before I lose it.

—Rita McAdam

The author says there was a truth she was "trying hard not to notice." In what circumstances have you tried not to notice the truth? How do you handle grief? Is your way constructive to your health and emotional well-being, or is it destructive?

Hurt and the holidays

December

One Christmas a dear friend sat beside me in an empty sanctuary. In the room below us we could hear the annual Christmas party concluding with exuberant carols. "I do not feel like singing happy baby Jesus songs," she said. Joyful celebrations are difficult when life is hurting. Two years ago near Christmastime, I wrote the following in my journal.

Home from church today and there is nothing to eat so we go to Arby's. The little waves have teased at me all morning and now they are getting bigger. Nelson comments as we eat, "You and Rhoda were having a good talk." Only I supply the name because he can't think of it. I know it is a question, but he never asks what we were talking about.

A small circle of friends were discussing a movie they had seen on TV about a husband caring for his wife who had Alzheimer's. We discussed how they experienced the movie and how I experience my reality.

"He has good days sometimes?" someone asked. I said I didn't even know how to answer that because sometimes when he has a good day it is a bad day for me. When he is feeling good and trying to be more independent, I must follow behind and clean up the mess and get him out of predicaments. The waves of sadness grew as I talked about my needs that I put aside because of his lost abilities and memory.

So what did he observe? I don't know. But on some level he must know I am sad. Now, I look out the window at Arby's as we eat in silence and I struggle with what is appropriate to say to him. I only know the hurt inside is too big to go without expression, so finally I say, "We were talking about a movie they saw about a woman with Alzheimer's."

Nelson doesn't respond, so I go on. "For whatever reason I'm feeling sad today. If I were you, I think I'd be throwing that sandwich across the room right now." His hands have a death grip on his sandwich and are shaking so that he cannot eat. Lettuce, tomato, and chicken are spilling onto the table. I say, "I'm glad you're not throwing things, though. Is there anything I can do to help?"

"If I put it down for a bit," he starts and then stops. I help pry his fingers loose and then reassemble the sandwich and hand it back to him. He takes it. All focus is on the sandwich. I feel a little better having acknowledged the waves of sadness washing over me. I can make it through lunch without a meltdown.

At home we settle in to finish the movie we started last night, *When a Man Loves a Woman*. I cry through most of it. Sideways glances at him give no clue that he is feeling anything but attentive, which in itself is a feat that he cannot always accomplish. After the movie, when he is watching a football game, I go to my bed, curl up in a fetal position, and let the tidal waves of grief come crashing in. Afterward I go for a walk.

That evening a pastor friend tells me we were all created to live in perfect relationship with God and others. We long for what is supposed to be, for what was meant to be. We search for it. We hurt when we do not have it. In the broken world gone awry from God's perfect creation, we suffer hugely for not being able to have what we legitimately want and need and what God means for us to have.

So here we are, in a world that feels like a big leaky boat. There are times when my faith tells me that God will ride out the storm with me, but there are as many times I am uncertain. How can God stand by and let the storm rage? Sometimes I am so intimidated by the storm that I am lost in sheer panic and it is only the prayers and faith of others that keep me believing God is with me at all.

Christmas is about hope, faith, and grace. I look back at what I wrote two years ago and acknowledge that holding on to hope and faith continues to be a struggle. But living with LBD has taught me how much I need grace from Nelson, my friends, family, God, and even myself. This much I can celebrate; I am given much grace.

I insulate myself because otherwise it hurts too much. So I just numb it down and forget about him as much as possible during the hours each day we're not together.

—Florrie Munat

My therapist said that rather than experiencing a loss, we are experiencing estrangement. Our spouses are still here, but they're not really.

—Jackie Moorhead

When has holding on to hope and faith ever been a struggle for you? What kept you going? Did you share your struggle with someone? Why or why not?

YEAR 11

The goal of wise grief is not to "get over" or "move on." The goal of wise grief is to learn from the experience. The goal is to integrate the experience into the fabric of our story. The goal is to live although grieving.
—Harold Ivan Smith[3]

3. Harold Ivan Smith, "You gotta be going there to get there." (*Journeys*, Hospice Foundation of America newsletter: October 2005), 2.

What is this terrible wrenching sadness that wraps around me each time I have had a house full of family and then go back to just the two of us? It is as if a little girl has been thrown to the wolves to fend for herself.

My heart demands to be heard, to break, to grieve, to spill its pain and sadness before I can move again into acceptance and belief that I am going to be okay, that the wolves of loneliness and fear will not destroy me, and that there is truly a Good Shepherd who will pick me up and carry me.—GHB

Change is the one constant

January

When Nelson was first diagnosed, he was put on Mira-pex along with other medications. It eliminated the middle-of-the-night vocal and physical outbursts that could cause him injury and jolt me from sleep into an adrenaline rush. I had heard a few years ago that this medication was not indicated for Lewy body dementia (LBD), but each time we tried to eliminate it, the outbursts returned.

Recently we began giving more Sinemet and tried again to eliminate the Mirapex. This time it worked, and now I am seeing a different Nelson.

It's a gray, rainy January day and we are sitting at breakfast when my drowsy silence is broken by Nelson asking, "Are you satisfied with our relationship?" My mind scrambles. Where is this going? While taking Mirapex, it often seemed that Nelson was here in body but not in soul. He seemed more often to function out of habit than from any inner resource.

Now, off the Mirapex, I have had more frequent glimpses of the old Nelson: the Nelson who responds to touch, the Nelson who wants to be an active participant in decisions and activities, and the Nelson who reaches out for connection. He can be more alert for brief periods. He also questions my decisions and choices. He offers solutions even though they are only partially informed because he can't hold the fistful of facts in his head that are needed to see the whole picture.

Am I satisfied with our relationship? I am suddenly awake. I don't know if I want to deal with where this might go. Carefully I choose words. "I think we have challenges that are very difficult to deal with—your LBD, my chemical sensitivities and chronic neck pain. I think that we have carved out a life that works pretty well."

He is silent. I wait. Then, when I feel my patience wearing thin, I ask, "What are you thinking?" He makes eye contact. He is focused. He has initiated this conversation. He speaks clearly, without a loss for words: "I want you to know how much I appreciate everything you do for us." The words sift down through many layers of grief and healing, resistance and acceptance, like a welcome blessing. They change everything and nothing. I am deeply moved and grateful, maybe even changed, but the disease marches on.

I have been hearing from a place deep inside: This could be as good as my life will ever get. Make it happy. I am trying to accept what he can give; and off the Mirapex, he can give a little more than before. I am trying to receive a back rub that is not what he once gave for what it is instead of always feeling the loss of what it is not.

It is another morning, and we wait for the bus that will take Nelson to adult daycare. He rises purposefully from his chair and moves toward the kitchen, suddenly stopping to turn toward me and ask, "What did I come out here for?" I laugh, imagining myself inside his brain and knowing all his thoughts.

"Honey, I have no idea," I tell him and then instruct him in our morning ritual. "Put your coat on." He does, unassisted—something he couldn't have done when he was on Mirapex. "Go open the garage door," I prompt.

"Where is the garage door?" This confusion is new and startles me.

Thinking that if he hears what he said repeated, it may help jog some clarity, I say, "You want to know where the garage door is?"

He looks at me. "If I go out there, I will find it?"

"Yes," I say. "If you go out there, you will find it." But I am not sure. With LBD you can never be sure. With LBD the only constant is change.

I was so looking forward to our retirement years because I loved being with my husband. He has always been such a loving husband and father. Now it is almost as though he is an empty shell.

—"Abigail"

A terrible weekend made me almost ready for the nursing home route, but recalling the "gaps" in care during the five years my mother was in a nursing home has made me pick myself up, dust myself off, and try to carry on at home a little longer.

—Verna Farr

A hallmark of LBD is vacillation in function. If you have ever experienced a situation when you didn't know what to expect, how did that affect you? How do you think that would add to the stress of the caregiver?

Living and managing life with LBD

February

Many times I've watched Nelson stand for long minutes in front of the mirror combing his thinning hair just before he goes to bed. I have done the reasonable and asked why. He has always ignored me. "It is just going to get messed up," I would tell him. He would continue to ignore me.

I finally get it. Dementia isn't reasonable. So this time I lean against the sink and watch and laugh but say nothing. "What?" he wants to know.

"You're combing your hair again right before you go to bed. I don't get it."

"That way I have a headstart in the morning." He smiles at himself in the mirror.

Not reasonable, I think. I laugh and say, "It makes no sense." He laughs too. We climb the stairs for bed, and as I lean down to tuck him in and kiss him goodnight, he grins. "Watch my hair." It is a challenge and a command. I kiss him and then put my hand on his head and give his hair a thorough tousle, hard and deliberate. His laugh bubbles out long and delighted. It is the kind I heard years ago when he would challenge someone to mischief and then participate wholeheartedly in it.

Another morning and the February sun shines brightly in the windows. I am cozily ensconced on the sofa in blankets and pillows. "Turn the lamp off, will you?" I ask. He is standing in the middle of the living room chewing peanuts, his breakfast of choice this morning, and he has a fistful in his hand. He hears my voice and shifts his focus to my face, but makes no move toward the lamp.

So I try again, this time pointing. He looks instead at the ceiling light and continues to chew. The pillows tell me this is still doable. "The lamp," I say, and jab my finger hard toward the corner. He looks at the ceiling again, then laughs. I know that laugh. It's a laugh that says, "I know I'm not doing something right, but I have no clue what it is." I spare us any further consternation and confusion, dig myself out of my nest, and turn off the lamp. I give him three pats on the shoulder, trying to reassure us both that it is okay.

It is closing in on time for his ride to daycare. He disappears into the closet, looking for a hat. He comes out wearing a visor. With the windchill, it is four degrees outside, so I eject myself again from the pillows and find his stocking cap and pull it onto his head while he says, "Watch my hair."

He stands by the window, watching for the bus. "I'm going to go pull down the garage door," he says.

"It's already down. You need to go pull it up." I know what he means. What demon possesses me to correct him? He sits down, confused.

"You need to go pull the garage door *up*." I say emphasizing the word, but the meaning eludes him. He looks at me as if I have lost my mind. I realize that to his ears I have just told him to do the very thing I have said is already done. I don't know how to dig myself out of this communication conundrum without confusing him further, so I say, "Just do what I say, and everything will be okay." He laughs. Multiple things go through my mind. He is a man. He needs to feel adequate. He needs his dignity. He wants to believe he can take care of others—not that someone must take care of him. While I am considering all this, he goes to the garage and opens the door.

Back inside he sits down to wait, then says something about one of the workers at daycare throwing away his plants. "They were just getting ready to bloom," he says wistfully when I question him. I listen to his disappointment, unable to sort out the reality, and say, "You should have thrown a tantrum." He looks at me with question marks in his eyes. I repeat myself and then say, "Have they ever seen a Nelson tantrum?" It's funny, and we both laugh. I can only think of one time in our forty years together that he has had what I would call a tantrum. He is more apt to shut down.

The bus is here. We hug goodbye, and another day is started. He goes off to live life, I to hold it together.

Later that night I put him to bed again. "You're getting pretty close to holy ground," he says as I lean down to kiss him. I look at him, puzzled. "You're getting pretty close to my hair."

It is wonderful to see how we can still have moments of intimacy and laughter among the really bad days.
—"LeeAnn"

When our grandson flew in, I told Grandpa that he was here. He replied, "You told me that last night." But by Saturday night, when our grandson and a cousin were trying to get him to bed, all hell broke loose. Grandpa, with fire in his eyes and fists flailing, yelled, "They are trying to get me to go to bed!" As he settled onto the toilet amid all the pandemonium, we waited outside the half-open door. Moments later Grandpa leaned forward and in a sweet little voice said, "Peek-a-boo." You can imagine the struggle we three had to keep from collapsing into shrieks of laughter.
—Verna Farr

Letting go of the reasonable and the logical is part of the adjustment for caregivers when someone is diagnosed with dementia. How difficult do you think this would be for you? Would you try to include the person with dementia in decision-making? How might you do that?

On the long road to acceptance

_____

March

It seems a lifetime ago that we were first confronted with the words "Lewy body dementia." At that moment, we began the long road to acceptance. At times the journey has been daunting. Chronicled here are memories along that road.

This morning Nelson asks if I am done with my cereal bowl. I am pleased that he is helping me clear the table—until he stands at the microwave ready to put the empty, unwashed bowl into it. How can one ever heal when the loss multiplies in front of your face?

How is it that he can turn the heater off when I am using it, but not turn off the lights after he uses them? How is it that he can pick a piece of lint from my clothes, but he cannot remember to turn off the water or flush the toilet? How is it that he can clear away the dish that I'm still using, but not push in his chair? Where is the sense of it?

A huge added challenge with LBD is the fluctuating cognition. He may be back today with higher function than yesterday, reminding you once again of how much has been lost and of happier times. You think you have adjusted to expecting less. But when capability spikes, you adjust and work with this new, higher function, knowing it can't last, but you get hooked into liking it. Then an hour or a day or a week later it's gone, and you face the same loss, the same grief, and the same letting go all over again.

The caregiver of a spouse with dementia must give up all rights to reason or negotiation in the relationship. There is no room for reasonable. There is only "this is the way it is and will be."

"Choose to fight it," or "choose to accept it." I go in and out of those two doors over and over again. And there are so many doors like them: doors that say "why me?" and "why not me?"; the door that reads "I can't do this any more" and the other one that says "I can and will do this." The doors are always open. I want to close the one that says "I can't accept this" and walk permanently through the "I will accept this" door. But about the time I think I have done that, I am thrown back into anger and pain and grief and am fighting my way back to the door of "acceptance."

It will never be my turn to be the one catered to in this relationship. It will never be my turn to let him cover the bases, fix the broken, cover my back, get our ducks in a row. Never. The door that says "my turn" is permanently closed.

The triggers are endless. A spousal caregiver has no shortage of triggers to work through. There is no counting on memory or comprehension to navigate a problem, no hope that the person beside you can pick up and carry life while you relax. It's not going to happen. The caregiver carries all his or her own baggage, and then must accept all of the spouse's baggage without qualification. If you don't, you unravel emotionally. Today I lost it, and now it's time to forgive myself and move on.

This morning I awake thinking about how the disease is like a kidnapper. It carries you off to a place where no one would go by choice. You feel violated and helpless, and you just want to go home, but home is not an option. Something bigger and more powerful is making the decisions for you. You are not consulted. You have limited, few, or no choices. You go along, if you so choose, out of commitment. You go out of love that takes on a different wardrobe than the one it wore when you were both healthy. You give yourself what you need when you can in order to continue in this relationship where love is costly.

The acceptance is like a greased watermelon. Just when you think you have a good hold, it slides to the floor and lies at your feet—messy, undone, and sweet but not very tempting. Do you want to try again? Or do you give up? Somehow I keep coming back to that endless supply of greased watermelons and try once more to hang on to the wholeness and the sweetness of greater acceptance.

You learn eventually. As a spousal caregiver you must change, or you will be filled with constant stress. So you give up your right to this or your preference for that, and you accommodate the malfunction of the person you care for. And if you are wise, you find other places and times to assert your own needs and wants.

When the moments and hours of acceptance come, you savor and enjoy them as best you can knowing that just around the corner is another challenge.

This morning Nelson says to me, "You take such good care of me." He acknowledges it, and I love him for it in that moment without the burden of regrets and heaviness. We have come a long, long way.

I know that I'm not the only spouse-caregiver who wants my husband, even for a day, to take over and get all of our "ducks in a row." I'd even settle for some of our ducks but that is beyond him. So I'm in charge of the ducks, the bills, the appointments, the home maintenance, and everything else—keeping everything in order by myself.

—Gayle Sobel

I struggle to muster the courage each day to face my parents' daily and personal challenges (my father with LBD and my mother with Alzheimer's) and their hesitation to accept that they can no longer live independently and away from family. When my dad is feeling scared and confused, I remind him that he was this little girl's first hero and still is.

—"Candice"

If someone you cared about were diagnosed with dementia would you move into acceptance permanently, or would you move in and out of it? What are some things you might do or tell yourself in an attempt to accept the diagnosis?

Word salad

April

"Word salad" is what some people call the scramble that happens when people with dementia substitute words and phrases for what they are actually trying to say. Word salads have been the source of both laughter and tears for us. The laughter comes with acceptance, when neither of us is overwhelmed with frustration or is under pressure. At other times it seems impossible to accomplish tasks, feel connection, or create understanding as words get hijacked and replaced by impostors, often without Nelson's awareness.

When I am coping well, word salads can be entertaining. We had stopped on our way out the driveway so that Nelson could pick up the mail. Getting back into the car, he wondered, "Can I tie myself up now?" This time I knew exactly what he meant. I had told him not to fasten his seatbelt when we left the house since I knew we would make a stop for the mail. He likes being the one to get out of the car and walk across the street for the mail. Such an easy translation lets me enjoy some amusement and move on.

Losing things like combs, gloves, and hats is routine (as is replacing them, because searching for them is frequently time-consuming and unproductive). One day when Nelson lost his glasses, he provided one of my favorite word salads. "My glasses dripped on the floor and now I can't find them," he told me. This time we found them easily, though not on the floor where he thought they had "dripped."

Nelson loves to take flowers from our garden to SarahCare, the adult daycare whose bus picks him up each morning. It was last spring at breakfast when we had this conversation:

"The bus is so hard to carry," he said.

"You aren't supposed to carry the bus," I countered, laughing at the image. He laughed too.

"The flowers are hard to carry on the bus?" I guessed, prompted by the flowers he had ready to go.

"Yes."

Some mornings the minutes tick slowly by while I wait for Nelson to accomplish some task. I stand waiting impatiently, wanting to do it for him, but he persists. As the disease progresses, he more frequently welcomes my offers of help. But there are still times when he needs to prove to himself or me that he can do it, and so I throw a straitjacket on my impatience and wait.

One such morning, Nelson simply couldn't sort out what to do with his shoes. When he was at last ready for me to help, he thrust his foot at me and said, "I forgot the middle foot."

"You have three feet now?" The image was startling, and we laughed together as I dropped to the floor to put his shoes on.

I often feel a mixture of sadness and amusement at the way words disobey his intentions. I have learned to focus on the amusement in the moment and deal with the sadness later by journaling, crying, talking to someone—whatever it takes to slosh through the emotions and move on.

Sometimes I can only hope I understand what Nelson intends to say. One morning I asked if anything had happened at SarahCare the day before to make him feel anxious, since during the night he had bolted out of bed.

Nelson thought about it, then began, "Two people do not . . ." There was a very long pause. I studied the ceiling, trying to reign in my impatience. Again he started but could not get past, "Two people do not . . ." I waited and studied something else. Finally he said, "They work against each other. Separately they are okay. When they are not all right, they are okay, if that makes sense." I gathered there was discord, but I did not know who or why. Sometimes even though my interest or curiosity is aroused, I simply have to accept that the information I have is enough.

On another morning, Nelson kept asking me if he could take the fan to "work." When I asked him to point at what he wanted to take, he pointed to the ceiling fan. I am not a morning person, and playing twenty questions first thing is not my idea of a good time, but sometimes it is the only way to get the information

I need. Eventually he said he didn't want to get his jacket wet. Eureka! It was raining outside. It was the umbrella he wanted. On that day in August, I journaled, "God, are you on this rollercoaster for sure and certain? If you're not, I'm bailing here and now."

Before Nelson started going to SarahCare full time, we would faithfully go to all of the Alzheimer's Association support group meetings. Somewhere along the way, he started calling it "old timers" because he couldn't remember "Alzheimer's." I ignored it at first, even though it irritated me terribly. I was closer to fifty than sixty at the time, and I was not at all happy to be in this group of late-sixty and seventy-year-olds. One day I erupted, "Don't call it old timers! I am not an old timer!" I knew it was pointless, but I drilled him on how to say "Alzheimer's."

Now we seem to be transitioning to the bigger challenge of more muffled, unintelligible patterns of speech. I can't let myself think about the days when that transition is complete. Instead, I remind myself of all those who have stayed with and supported me on this rollercoaster. It is because of them I can say I haven't bailed. I am still here deciphering word salads, living on the rollercoaster, and praying often for help to hang on, and for the wisdom to know how to cope as the disease progresses.

My favorite word salad is when my husband asked me, "Are you still going to ovaries?" After some confusion, I finally figured out he meant "Curves."

—Florrie Munat

When my dad forgets what he is saying, he always says, "My train has jumped off its tracks." We all giggle.

—"Jill"

She was a physicist but when she talked about quantum mechanics and theory she pretty much lost her audience. That's when I noticed the "salad vocabulary." Soon after that, her ability to speak was severely restricted. That's when I really felt I was alone and losing her as my lifelong companion.

—"Seth"

When a caregiver is trying to accomplish a task, it can be harder to see the humor in difficult communication. When are you least able to see the humor in mistakes others make? How good are you at letting a task be secondary to a relationship? What kinds of situations do you think would make word salads most intolerable for you?

Respite and the re-entry blues

May

Sometimes I collect moments like precious gems to horde in my memory for revisiting when I need a break from the demands of caregiving. This month I collected and savored a few.

Today a college kid told me repeatedly how much he liked the flower arrangement I brought to church. We rarely speak. Our paths are worlds apart. His compliment was the first gem of my day.

Tonight I received the second gem when a friend asked how I was doing and was able to listen and be with me as I described the emotional tangle I felt during the past week. Her hug was like an island of respite in that moment—a place to cry, be weak, be needy, and still be received. She said she doesn't know what to do to help. I said, "You are doing it."

"Often," I told her, "people ask me how Nelson is doing. I need to talk about how I am doing, but that invitation is rarely given." It's understandable. Few people want to invite the pain or know what to do with it.

Eric called tonight, and that was a third gem, as hearing from either of the kids always is.

When another friend called, that was a fourth. I can tell her anything and know that she will not advise or judge, but will listen, reflect, and support.

I helped Nelson get into bed after finding him asleep half in and half out. He said, barely audibly, "It was a busy day. You did a good job." I think that might be another gem, but at the same time I note that his dependency on me is growing and that he more frequently assumes my help. I collect that moment, unsure if I will be able to savor it.

With time, I recognize that I need more restorative time and have created spaces for walks, lunches, and time with friends. These times in relationship with others have been islands of connection and emotional comfort. Now, as the disease takes more of Nelson from me, I find myself needing greater support, connection, conversation, and presence from others in order to do the necessary caregiving.

Today, I recognize that I need more moment-collecting to keep me going. I have returned from four days away. I left numerous sticky notes with information for Nelson's multiple caregivers. Since Nelson didn't want to go into a care facility for the one night when other options weren't available, I had to be firm in my resolve to leave home. Scheduling was tricky and transitioning between caregivers was complicated. I felt guilty as I made plans and packed. For the first time, I was going to see where our son lives, and I was leaving Nelson behind. I silenced the voice of guilt with the voice of reason and the validation of others. "Go," they said. "You need it."

In between what seemed like monumental efforts to prepare to go, and then returning to caregiving blues, I enjoyed an absolutely fabulous four days of rest, relaxation, companionship, renewal, and laughter. I spoke, and there was feedback. No one fell asleep in the middle of my sentences. I listened, and nothing was garbled or incomprehensible. Conversation flowed freely. I got up in the morning and went to bed in the evening with no one depending on me to monitor dressing or pill-taking or grooming. For four whole days I felt normal and whole again.

Now I am home, and caregivers send emails to assure me that everything went well. I understand all the reassurances, but my beleaguered caregiver self wonders why it goes "well" for others and seems so hard for me. I want to hear them say they can't understand his words. I want to know they too found it difficult to keep him oriented or on task. I want to know that I am not alone in the way LBD affects me.

This morning as he clears the table, I am still eating breakfast. "That's my spoon," I say. "Leave it there."

"What about broccoli?" he asks.

Yes, I have the re-entry blues. My sister suggests I start working on my next getaway. She's right, I think. I will have to start building anticipation into my respite and re-entry routine. Otherwise, re-entry becomes daunting, and gem collecting loses its power to give solace.

At the beach, I remember thinking about why I was allowed the privilege of this nice little vacation, why I was at the ocean while he was sitting in a small room in a nursing home, and then yelling at the waves, "Because I can!" I was just dripping with guilt.

—Florrie Munat

More and more he is confused, and the frustrations are so hard to adjust to. I keep expecting him to understand like he used to, but on "bad" days he just can't.

—"Claire John"

A well spouse is sometimes referred to as the invisible victim of a disease. Does "inviting the pain" keep you from asking how a caregiver is doing? Why?

Banish the Judge

June

This morning Nelson is at home instead of at daycare so that he can go with me to Columbus for the Area Agency on Aging caregiver awards ceremony. I and eleven others from around the state will be given an award. But now I am stressed because he is at loose ends until we leave at 1:00. I prefer him to be at SarahCare, out of my way. This is when the inner voice of the Judge appears to suggest that I do not deserve this award. The Judge is here, waiting to pounce on my every caregiver thought and decision.

I spent a whole day looking for just the right clothes to wear to the awards ceremony; now I feel guilty for not finding him a new outfit. Shopping with him takes a kind of courage I couldn't muster then. Besides, Nelson often says he has too many clothes. The Judge does not care what Nelson says.

"Why do I feel guilty?" I ask myself this morning

"Because it is the only decent thing to do," the Judge says.

Last night Nelson collected rocks to paint. I told him I would rather he paint them at SarahCare where he got the idea during crafts time.

I feel guilty that I don't choose to work with him on such projects at home. Then I remember what twelve years has taught me. "I have limits," I tell the Judge. "That's how I've survived—by accepting my limits."

The Judge must go. If the Judge has not been happy in all these years, the Judge will never be happy. I will not give her an audience. I banish her by speaking Truth. I am not God. I cannot get it right every time. I cannot be perfect, as much as I or others might want me to be. I need to be human. I am doing the best I can. I have been here for Nelson. I have given more than a decade to caregiving. I will not degrade the effort by giving them to the Judge.

Don had three falls in the bathroom but didn't hurt himself. Naturally I am not supposed to let him fall—good luck. Right now I want to strangle that inner judge. Thank goodness tomorrow is a new day as I'm ready to put this one to rest.

—*"Beth"*

I need a break but I have a very short distance I can go because [my mother] is always in need or calls for me when she can't see me. The laundry room is my crying room. Does anybody ever feel like running away and never coming back? I'm sure you do if

you're human, but we are all good people and have a
bad case of the guilts.

—"Amanda"

In what areas do you accept your limitations? In
what areas do you take on guilt? How might you
continue to love yourself as you are while making
changes to improve yourself?

.

Visiting the memories

July

When I give Nelson a haircut or wash his hair in the shower, he can't keep his head upright. I'm constantly pushing against his forehead to move him into an erect position. Looking at him with his head erect and his back straight, I have flashbacks of the old Nelson. I've been looking at the top of his head for so long that I have forgotten what he once looked like and how handsome he was.

I am trying to consolidate and organize photo albums that have accumulated over the years. There are so many memories.

The first picture I ever had of Nelson was a school picture he gave me. I took it with me to camp where I was a counselor, and the girls in my cabin giggled and squealed over his good looks. My heart beat a little faster each time I looked at it.

I was so full of knowing and hope then. I believed that when we were together everything would be okay and that life could not be better once the miles between Ohio and Michigan no longer separated us. I believed his chiseled features, easy presence, good humor, and mop of curly hair were all I'd ever need.

I look at that picture now, and the same heart-stirring fondness comes roaring over me with the strength of a locomotive. Only now the engine carries with it carload after carload of loss. The once articulate storyteller cannot put forth his words. The entertainer now looks to me for a script. The adventurer is on an LBD leash. The risk-taker must have a caregiver who is not. The intelligent and adept teacher cannot access information. The cuddler is rigid. The strong, enthusiastic baritone can't read the hymnal words fast enough. The father who once told his little girl that he could fix anything needs help with everything.

Looking forward with hope and promise is necessarily a right of the young. Perhaps wading in loss is the passport to maturity and wisdom. Dr. Keith Ablow says the more we try to distance ourselves from the pain, the farther down the road to nowhere we will get.[4] So I will visit past memories as I can and wade through present loss as I must. It is the path of a caregiver who wants to avoid going nowhere.

---

4. From a television interview, used with permission of Dr. Ablow.

*The invitation to my fiftieth high school reunion
is sitting on my desk. I've made airline and hotel
reservations. Can I go alone? I too want to avoid
going nowhere, so I will buy the ticket and mail in
the reply to the invitation.*

—"Beth"

What memories in your life do you avoid? What do
you lose or gain by avoiding them?

Living with the dissonance dragon

September

This morning I am feeling the weather. Or is it reality that floods over me and wants to pull me under?

Last night, Nelson was, for the first time in weeks (or was it months?), awake all evening and attentive when I spoke. He even fed himself.

It precipitated a subtle change in me. I enjoyed an audience for my thoughts. I spoke of all the different things I'd learned from the four heating contractors I interviewed. He almost seemed to be taking it in. He was here. I wasn't talking to space.

I gave him his shower. When I tucked him in bed, he invited me to stay. He wanted to talk.

He told me that the social worker at daycare talked with him and "Tania" about what is appropriate for their relationship. He smiled and said, " 'Tania' kept saying, 'Are we in trouble? Are we in trouble?' "

I saw the fondness for her on his face. I was relieved that the conversation went well. I said, "And you can still be friends."

He said, "Yes."

It seems a nice resolution to a relationship that is serving a need but causing him to be concerned about what is right.

I lay beside his shakiness and felt the familiar dichotomy of my life. It pulls me in opposite directions. I was relieved and happy for him but I was confounded for us as we both try to meet our relationship needs.

I had a little more of him last night than the night before and am thankful and uplifted. But experience has taught me that this will be short-lived. Knowing that, it is difficult to celebrate the moment.

This morning he is confounded by every need. I can't understand his words. He can't follow my directions. We move ahead until he is dressed and ready for his ride to daycare. He seems to be in purposeless motion. He can't verbalize his intentions.

I invite him to the garden. I want to show him the unseasonable blooms of an amaryllis. He totters. His unsteadiness is unusual, and I look for a cane. We make our way to the garden. He shows no sign of surprise or wonder, no consternation, and no registered response to what would have at one time lit up his face and elicited exclamations. When I suggest that we return to the house, he mutters an agreeable sound, but starts off in the opposite direction. I steer him back. When the daycare bus arrives, he asks what it is doing here. I tell him, "This is Monday. You go to

SarahCare today." I can only wonder what trick his mind has played on him this time.

The day sprinkles further discord into my thoughts when a male acquaintance showers me with compliments and presses to take me to lunch. I decline but later observe that I have a vulnerable longing for companionship. I am pulled apart by longing and commitment.

I want to slay the dissonance dragon that breathes its stinging breath into our relationship and haunts my prayers. "God, how can you create us with needs and then watch our suffering inability to meet them?" The question hangs in the air between us.

I see my mom's loneliness and wish I could fill it with more love. She's tired; her garden is not the pride it was once.

—"Rachel"

We had a couple of bad days last week when Chuck couldn't stand. His speech was almost inaudible and unclear. When I read to him, he'd fall asleep after two sentences. Then after two days of this, he was standing again (which means he can leave the nursing home), speaking more clearly, and listened to me read for an hour.

—Florrie Munat

In what circumstances have you been pulled apart by "longing and commitment"? Did your fear of judgment from others influence your choice? Are there questions that "hang in the air between you and God"? What are they?

Tug of war

October

Nelson was gone, visiting his family in Michigan. Did I miss him? Yes. Did I enjoy the freedom and change? Yes.

Several years ago I went to an auto supply store and asked if I could buy the paper mats that mechanics leave in your car. They sold me a pack of two hundred and fifty. I began using them in place of rugs on the bathroom floors. Accidents are easy to spot, and the mats work as blotters, usually making cleanup easier. Since they are disposable, I am not constantly washing floors or rugs. But the mats are also ugly and cold.

Soon after Nelson left for Michigan, I threw out the mats that had been down and put rugs in their place. For four days I walked into the bathroom to the great sensation of warmth and comfort on my feet.

With Nelson gone, I joined friends, a married couple, in a hike through hickory and beech trees that were beginning to drop their fall foliage. It was exhilarating to walk without energy limitations imposed by LBD. It was liberating to converse without repetition, careful enunciation, and repeated explanations. Still, I was joining a busy husband and wife. "You sure you don't need this time just for you?" I had asked. They assured me it was okay.

We came upon "chicken of the woods," a fungal growth on trees. It was a real find to these naturalist friends, she being an enthusiastic high school biology teacher. Nelson would have loved the bright colored orange tops and yellow undersides on the petal-shaped brackets running like shelves up opposite sides of the tree. He would have tasted this novelty with us later and, if he liked it, would have probably eaten more than his share. If he didn't like it, when offered more he would have said, "Maybe tomorrow."

I sat at the counter in their kitchen and watched as our friends blended their movements and enthusiasm at the stove: "Try this . . ."; Let's get . . ."; "Okay, I have . . ."; "Where is the . . ." Their synchronized movements were testimony to their years of marriage, companionship, and healthy minds. I was aware of the stark contrast to my own life.

I tasted the "chicken." It was deliciously moist and flavorful and, yes, tasted like chicken. Nelson, the science teacher, who once ate large, toasted Columbian ants while his students chanted "Go Mr. B!" would have loved the whole experience, but Nelson of LBD would have been tired by this time and ready for home.

Later that day, I went to a viewing following the death of a friend's father. Sandwiched in line with strangers in front and behind, I wanted Nelson at my side. I wanted the comfort of the familiar, someone to hold on to. Mutual friends, two couples, had already been through the line and were speaking together in a small, companionable group that made me feel even more alone. This is what it is like to be single, I thought. I did not like it.

Now Nelson is at home. The paper mats are back on the floor. His muted voice and lack of words crush my interest in communication. Still we go for a walk and I have his company. He stumbles on a root, falls to the ground, and rolls like a teddy bear, then jumps up laughing.

I am in the middle of an emotional tug-of-war, alone and feeling single one minute, together and married with difficult and broken connections the next. There is nothing to be done but review my commitment, acknowledge whichever end of the emotional tug-of-war I need to process now, and pray that I can get on with caregiving.

Maurice is eighty-five, in very good physical shape, but barely able to get from bed to chair and chair to bathroom. I just turned seventy-eight and recently said to the doctor, "I think he will live forever!" She said, "No, not forever," and I replied, "But it's my forever!"

—Verna Farr

I had a rather strange feeling when a long-time friend lost her husband this week after a short illness. I was sad for her, but at the same time I felt like that should have been me. I rather envied her the short period of waiting. It sounds like I want him to die, but that is not the case. I just find the waiting hard.

—"Beth"

I am constantly hearing about how draining motherhood is and how they need help to keep them from depression. Never a word about long-term caregivers. Like we are just a throw-away part of society. They really don't know what to do with us.

—Rita McAdams

Spousal caregivers deal with a unique kind of grief. While the loved one is there physically, his ability to be in relationship gradually disappears. The caregiver is left in limbo. How do you think you would handle this in-between place? What would you require of yourself in commitment to your spouse if the disease lasted ten years? Fifteen years? Twenty years? Would you pursue another relationship where emotional needs might be better satisfied?

Giving thanks

November

We went for a hayride in an autumn wood where yellow gold leaves shimmered on beech trees in early evening sunlight. When the ride was over, the people around Nelson gave patient hands and long minutes of assistance as he unsteadily climbed from the middle of the hay wagon. As we stepped down into scattering leaves, I felt blessed by our friends' easy acceptance and offers of help. For this, I am thankful.

We have a son and a daughter who are both living in other states. I've heard it said, a family is as sick as its sickest member. The impact of my chemical sensitivities and of Nelson's dementia radiates out to our children, our extended families, and our friends. Everyone touched in any way copes, changes, grows, and adjusts in the best way they know and can. For our children, who continue to forgive my failures, and who have changed and grown with me in this unplanned journey, I am thankful. For our extended families that have gracefully lived in the shadow of our diseases and grief, I am thankful. For all who have suffered loss and still been willing to sit with ours, I am thankful.

Years ago, before LBD was in our vocabulary, my younger sister, who lives out of state, began working in the field of dementia, providing leadership for coordination of education and services on a state level. Now, every third weekend she and her husband give us a hand with home repair or lawn care. More importantly, they give respite not just from the caregiving but from the loss of reciprocity of relationship that I feel so profoundly. Their visits keep me from falling off the edge of sanity, and keep me believing that even now after twelve years, I can still carry on. For this I am thankful.

Nelson's temperament is such that he will laugh at his own confusion. When his tongue refuses to make words come out in any sensible pattern, he seems to find it entertaining. When I make a feeble joke at my own impatience, he will laugh spiritedly. When there is no explaining some behavior that I have called to his attention, at best, he is likely to grin sheepishly and look at me with puzzlement. At worst, he ignores me. He does not put out the combativeness or aggression that plagues some caregivers. I know that I can be very thankful for this.

There have been times in the last twelve years of LBD that I simply could not dig deep enough to find any faith or feel any comfort that God was with us in this disease. For many years I couldn't sing "Great Is Thy Faithfulness." How could a faithful God let me struggle with my own isolating health issues and then let me lose my husband to another isolating and horrendous disease? I would sit biting back the tears of frustration as others sang with what seemed to me to be unflinching confidence.

The struggle isn't over. I seem to hold God's goodness in one hand and feelings of betrayal and abandonment in another. It's where I am, and I've accepted that as the condition of my humanity for now. For those who have spoken their own doubts and faith struggles aloud to me, I am thankful. For those who hold fragile faith as enough, who have given me the gift of their strength and weakness, I am thankful.

This is a journey I didn't plan to take in my life, but I've finally accepted it. Now I tell people that my mother has become the daughter I never had.
—Diana Blackstone-Helt

I just seem out of it most of the time. Can't seem to get a grip on things and feel things are swirling out of control. Been making some bad decisions and not reacting normally to things. Finally made a call to arrange for some help before I lose it.
—Rita McAdam

What difficult situation have you experienced that challenged your faith or your ability to be thankful?

A caregiver's Christmas list

December

My Christmas list is short. Things, it seems, are what I have too much of. I can't keep track of all mine, all his, and all ours. I am trying, not very successfully, to pare down the number of things that need organizing, dusting, fixing, storing, filing, displaying, accounting for, or maintaining. So, beyond a very short list of things, my Christmas list is this:

I would like to have patience for all the times I need to stop what I'm doing to focus on listening and deciphering the vanishing voice of my husband. I need patience, too, for finding the lost things: my glasses that show up on his face, his wallet that surfaces in his underwear drawer, his glasses that lived for weeks with his boots in the garage. Just wrap up patience with a bow that promises tranquility on those days when I seem to run out of the inner resources that being a caregiver requires.

I would like before-breakfast endurance. When I want only to put my feet to the morning floor and stretch slowly toward the day but, instead, need to bolt into attentiveness and vigilance to avoid messes, misses, and moroseness, then I need endurance. When I get up in the morning and want to remember my dreams but instead am instantly needed for unraveling his tangled intentions, then I need endurance.

I would like to live with hope again instead of this gnawing knowing that nothing I do is going to bring back my husband's vitality and nothing is going to stop this slow shuffle of decline and loss. I would like to have a faith that doesn't waver with my circumstances, that believes with the certainty that God is in this picture.

I fantasize that ABC might do a show called *Extreme Care for the Caregiver*. I see a crew of resources coming to the doors of caregivers and announcing that "help is on the way." We caregivers are tired enough and most of us are old enough that we wouldn't be able to jump up and down and scream our delight for the cameras. Perhaps we could faint or collapse from exhaustion.

Since no one can fulfill this list for me, and ABC is not at my door, I will ask for hugs. Nelson's hugs are diluted by dementia and need, his strong arms weakened by disease. I miss those attentive hugs. Just give me hugs for Christmas, strong reassuring hugs that tell me someone close to me cares.

My husband has been disintegrating before my eyes for seven years and for more than thirteen years dealing with chronic health problems. My belief in God's purpose, my family, and my sense of humor get me through day and night.

—"Irene"

If you have you ever struggled with your faith because of a difficult loss, what was it like? Were you open to others about your struggle? If so, how did they respond? Were they helpful? If not, what would have been helpful? If you weren't open to others about your struggle, why not?

YEAR 12

The most painful state of being is remembering the future,
particularly the one you can never have.
—Source unkown

I miss him, but he is here.

I am homesick, but I am at home.

I want to be catered to, but I am the caterer.

I want to be with someone, but I already am,
and he is not here.

If you don't let go of the memories and you keep fighting the
little stuff—the constant, ongoing, ever present, little stuff—
you can never have peace.

It's a constant giving up of the way it should have been
and could have been
to accepting
what is.

—GHB

My new year

—————

January

Someone asked me if I had made any New Year's resolutions. I laughed, surprised that it hadn't even occurred to me. Maybe, I thought, it is because it is all I can do to stay focused on my intentions.

I intend to live caring for myself. When my life requires more of me than I feel I have to give—in those moments when Lewy body dementia (LBD) flaunts banners at me that shout "You are not enough!"— then I will give to myself until I have enough. When I lose me, I am lost to everyone.

So I will put the oxygen mask on me first. I will acknowledge the tears in my eyes first. I will turn the light on in my soul first. I will find a place to rest my weariness. I will ask me how I'm doing and will look for a place to renew when I need it. I will listen to my own heart first. I will ask, seek, and knock until I am filled to more than "enough." I will give from the over-flow. That is my intent.

I intend to live loving my children. It takes my breath away when I think of my children carving their way in a world that is changing so fast and has so many pitfalls. I know they too will need to have enough. I want to package "enough" and give it to them, but that's not the way it works. So I want to forge ahead listening, mirroring, questioning, and reminding them that, no matter what, they are loved and in my eyes they will always be enough.

I intend to live with commitment to Nelson. Even though much of him is lost to this tedious LBD decline, I want to be worthy of his trust. It sounds noble and it is, I suppose. But noble intentions get easily lost in daily tests of tenacity.

I intend to live believing in the goodness and mercy of God. When life seems to shatter me, I intend to let my searching soul pick up the pieces of my life and hold them before God for inspection. I intend to let the quivering voice of doubt be enough when that's all I can muster. When my question to God "Why have you forsaken me?" presses, I intend to speak my questions truthfully. I intend to be unapologetic and joyful when faith carries me.

I intend to live in a community of friends and family where my life intentions get tumbled, tested, and worn smoother under the scrutiny of others. I intend to live compassionately in a world community and gently on a stressed planet.

These are the intentions that define my life. Often I lose sight of them, ignore them, and fight them. Then I come back to them to build on, fortify, refine, and redefine their application. If, in the murky fog of the coming year, I can live more consistently by my intentions, the year will be a successful one.

My life verse is Isaiah 41:10 where God promises to always be with us and to strengthen us and to never leave us or forsake us.

—"Juanita"

What intentions do you use as a compass for your life?

Struggle and hope

February

I keep trying to hang on to the goodness in life; I keep trying to focus on the hope. Still, it seems, I'm on a leash that will let me go only so far toward equanimity before I am jerked back to my reality and the grief of struggle.

At times I am able to focus away from LBD and its consequences and get absorbed in the good I am able to create in our lives. In those times I can laugh at LBD absurdities: the undershirt he is trying to pull up as shorts, or the nonsensical word salads that come out of his mouth. I enjoy life in spite of the disease.

Then something happens. I am tired, tasks oriented, or just want an easy relationship and comfort. Then suddenly I am back to a familiar and unwelcome place where the yoke of an LBD marriage pulls me down into a cesspool of grieving.

I am in partnership with someone who cannot pull his weight. I arrange and manage life for two people.

Lewy body has taken away our equilibrium. He counts on me to organize and schedule our agenda for him, barely aware that if my ability goes away, we will surely both be in a heap of trouble.

Meanwhile, I live my life in a sort of limbo, a no man's land, not as a single person and not feeling the relational benefits of a marriage. Must I just be strong and live out all the pretty "shoulds" without contention?

I "should" be strong and committed to the relationship with my husband of forty years, and that relationship "should" sustain me. I require myself to surrender to my commitment, but how long can I swallow my loneliness?

I "should" be able to focus on the good in my life. When I am focused on friendships, family support, and new experiences, I am energized. Then, in my joy and enthusiasm, I turn around to share it, but the excitement falls on barely comprehending ears and elicits muddy LBD questions with long pauses that drain away my desire to engage. Then I am jerked back into struggling against the losses.

I "should" shift my focus to people and places other than myself and my circumstances. So, I push my comfort zone and surrender to going places that will give me new experiences. There I meet new people and am teased with new relationships that look more satisfying than the one I am committed to at home. Then I am brought again full force into grief.

For more than a decade we have been a partnership: Nelson, LBD, and I. It has been a struggle that seems to require frequently revisiting a realization described by Joan D. Chittister in *Scarred by Struggle, Transformed by Hope.*

"There is no one, I come to realize with a kind of empty shock, on whom I can depend to do my bidding this time. Despite the network of people I have carefully constructed over the years, there is no one with connections enough to pull this final string for me. There is no one on earth, no matter how well-disposed they may be to me, who can make the inevitable go away. It is like losing at the Supreme Court of life."[5]

While I may feel I have lost at the Supreme Court of life, I will not lose more by giving up on the potential for me to experience greater acceptance and hope.

Yesterday, February 14, Nelson sang a valentine song to me that he learned in kindergarten. "Valentine, Valentine, tell me what you say. I love you. I love you, more and more each day."

I just couldn't resist saying, "So you saved it all these years to sing it to me standing naked in the bathroom door." We shared a laugh and a hug.

I believe with all my heart that he should be home; however, my mother does not feel like she can handle all of this, so she insists on keeping him there. He often cries when he sees me and tells me it means the world to him that I come. I am the daughter

---

5. Joan D. Chittister, *Scarred by Struggle, Transformed by Hope* (Grand Rapids: Wm. B. Eerdmans, 2003), 57.

here, not the spouse, and maybe I don't see this
clearly.

—"Andrea"

Help me understand what's happening to my mom
who doesn't speak too much about what's happening
to her marriage as a result of LBD.

—"Lelah"

What would commitment look like for you in a
marriage that included ten or more years of dementia?
To what extent would "shoulds" influence you?

A longing and a gift

June

It was a sunny day and we had stopped at a garage sale. It's an activity that we can share and enjoy together. A framed picture caught Nelson's eye and he wanted to buy it but I resisted. In all our years of of marriage, we have collected so much. What would we do with all of our stuff? What would we do with yet another picture? He persisted and I stalled. "Where would we put it?" He wasn't deterred. I gave in.

That evening we sat side by side on the sofa looking at the picture of a fishing village. I asked him about the picture and what he liked about it. Once a great storyteller, he struggled to communicate. "The people on this boat are praying for safety before they go out." There was a long pause before he pointed to a lone man standing on the dock. "He wants to go out too but his family won't let him."

"Why won't they let him?" I asked, knowing how hard it was for him to accept the many times "no" had come his way in the last few years.

"It is too dangerous." There was another long pause. I thought about the things Nelson had been told he could no longer do because of the disease. No shingling a roof. No climbing ladders or driving a car. So many things he loved had been taken away. "He is feeling sad," Nelson concluded. It was as if all of his own longings for what he could once do were embodied in that lonely man on the dock.

"You must really identify with him," I reflected. "All that adventure out there but your family says you can't go because it's too dangerous." He nodded.

There was another long pause, and then he pointed off to the side where a small group of children watched from the shore. "They can't go either." We sat for a long time just feeling the losses and the loneliness of this disease and each wrestling with our private grief and questions. How do you see God in so much loss? Does God care?

As we prepared for bed, Nelson pointed out some unidentified itchy bites on his leg. A few phone calls later, we decided to visit the emergency room. After treatment for spider bites, we crawled into bed in the middle of the night exhausted.

The next day was Sunday, and though we were tired we kept our usual routine and went to church. Nelson found his place as greeter while a friend approached me. He had been given tickets, he said, for a day fishing trip. If it was okay with me, he would invite Nelson. We talked about some concerns. I knew the friend was well aware of Nelson's needs and would be watchful of him, so I agreed to the invitation.

After church I watched Nelson playing a game of four square with a group of children on the church basketball court and thought how his life had been reduced to playing with children and watching others his age venture out. It was then that my sleep-deprived brain remembered the picture! Children and a lonely old man were left behind; Nelson had felt their longing and verbalized it to the best of his ability. I felt a surge of reassurance and joy. God was reminding us that we were not in this alone. He was watching! Nelson was about to step off the dock!

The fishing trip was a great success. Though dementia often robs him of his short-term memory, he has not forgotten that he caught the biggest fish of all, a twenty-seven-inch walleye. In the freezer it is testimony to the truth of his adventurous fish story as well as a reminder that this journey is not taken alone.

When Chuck talked about "coming home," I don't think he was really asking to come back home and live. I think he was saying with the only words he had available to him that he wanted to go back in time and have his old life back. I wanted that, too.
—Florrie Munat

What stories in your life are reminders that you are not alone?

The communication conundrum

July

I have laughed, cried, felt helpless, hopeful, and happy as I have shared my personal stories with other caregivers and heard theirs. Connecting with other caregivers is an antidote to the isolation and loss that nips at my heels. Knowing their stories fends off the loneliness caused by lack of meaningful communication with Nelson.

My conversations with Nelson, if you can call them that, range from the ludicrous to the normal. Nelson's hushed tones and inability to articulate clearly are taxing for both of us. We have lost a crucial tool for connecting. Still, the nature of the disease gives us interludes of togetherness when I can receive them for what they are rather then reject them for what they are not.

"We have a treat!" I say one day, knowing Nelson's appetite for sweets.

"Whose retreat?" he asks. I consider this. I could use one, but maybe now isn't the time to say so. Timing is everything, they say.

"How about we give you a shower?" I am feeling him out to see if he's alert and willing enough for the process.

"What green thing?" he asks.

I decide the shower can wait.

We are in the bathroom when he picks up my razor. I reach out and take it saying, "No, that's mine."

"Well, then where is yours?" he says. My mind seems toyed with. It laughs. It cries. It protests. It gives up.

They say you are supposed to speak slowly, enunciate, have them looking at you. We are both movers. I could probably save myself a lot of grief if I stopped moving, faced him, got his attention, and then spoke slowly with good enunciation. But does anybody really do that? All the time? I should try. See what happens.

I would do it if there were an emergency, wouldn't I? I should get in the habit now.

"Slow down. There is no fire," I say one day to him when his body is moving faster than his mind.

"Where?" he asks alarmed. Okay. I get it. Get his attention. Don't speak on the run. Enunciate. Speak slowly.

"I beg to bicker with you," he says one day.

"You want to bicker with me about what?" I ask.

"I forget." He laughs and I join him. Dementia does give me that. He can't hold a grudge if he can't remember it. Sometimes, there are small blessings with dementia if we look hard enough.

Having lived with someone for forty years makes communication easier. I know his code. When he says, "Do you want to see Jim today?" I know he means that *he* wants to see Jim today.

"How would you like some oatmeal?" means "I want some oatmeal."

No matter how smudged his glasses are, if I ask if they need to be cleaned, he will say, "They're good."

Or asked if he wants to do something, he will rarely say no. Instead he will say, "Maybe tomorrow," which really means no.

Then from time to time just to keep us guessing, this crazy disease throws in some normalcy. He asks me very clearly where we were getting the money to put in the new furnace. Wanting to reassure him so that he doesn't worry, but knowing he won't be able to understand Medicaid "spend down" formulas and other complicated explanations, I wave my hand nonchalantly, grin, and say, "Oh, we have plenty of money!"

He looks at me smiling and just as clearly says, "You don't leave me anything to worry about."

Sometimes communication actually does what it is supposed to!

I am crying [for] help and can't seem to make anyone, not even the doctors, understand. I am going to try again. One more doctor. I can't take it anymore.

—Pat Smith

*As much as family and friends try, they really don't
"get it." They can't understand when he seems so
"with it," making a valiant attempt at normalcy, that
it is exhausting and unsustainable.*

—Christine Greig

How do you respond when communication breaks
down in a significant relationship? How do you
think you would handle the loss of communication
that accompanies dementia?

Lost power

August

Hurricane Ike reached his tempestuous tentacles all the way up to Ohio, and on a Sunday evening at 8:30 we found ourselves without power. I had anticipated the possibility and had small amounts of water and a four-battery flashlight. With my pioneer heart and long ago camping experience, I felt prepared and unalarmed. Besides, the power would be back on soon, I thought.

We are on well water, so I rationed out what was stored in the pipes of our old nine-foot, floor-to-ceiling house. Tap on to get fingertips wet. Tap off. Soap the fingertips. Tap on for a two-second rinse. Tap off. We did this for the first morning. That day I bought a dispenser of baby wipes and, supplementing our needs with those, we never ran out of water at any of our faucets. It was like the biblical woman and her oil. I kept thinking that each time we used it would be the last, but it kept coming, even after one of us would forget and turn on the tap as if there were an endless supply.

Early the next morning we received a phone call. Adult daycare would not be open. My experience with camping didn't coincide with my experience with dementia, but I had a couple of errands to run. In a car Nelson is either entertained or lulled to sleep. I stretched the errands to include lunch with my sister and her husband, who also were without power.

One of the errands was to stop at my friend Jane's house (she had power) and pick up a battery-operated lantern. This was to take the place of three nightlights—one near Nelson's bed, one in the hall, and one in the bathroom. I slept better that second night, knowing we had more than the full moon to illuminate trips to the bathroom. Still, minimal light adds to dementia's nighttime confusion, and cleaning up bathroom misses without water and good light is at the top of my avoid-when-possible list. My pioneer spirit was wavering, but still I never questioned that the power would be back.

On day two I struck gold! I remembered the spigot at the bottom of the hot water heater. One screwdriver turn and I had a pan of clear tepid water for washing dishes. Then, at my sister's house, the power came back on, and they offered us their generator. For several hours that afternoon, we fired up their generator to do laundry and get the freezer and fridge back on track. We stepped over power cords strung through the house, endured the exhaust, and listened to the heartbeat of the generator that made it all possible.

After three nights and almost three days, the power came back. We now have a seemingly unlimited supply of water. The lights in every corner illuminate the evening routine and accommodate nighttime needs. The refrigerator is doing its job. The toilets flush. We are able to return to our normal.

If only we could know that someday the lights will come back on for Nelson. But those are electrical circuits that no power company in the world can fix. Those are connections that we have no hope in our lifetime of repairing. Ike was a huge inconvenience. But inconvenience doesn't begin to describe the impact that LBD brings to the human brain and experience.

A few hours before the power came back, I watched a convoy of trucks bearing our electric company's insignia roll by our home. I felt a surge of hope and relief just knowing they were finally in the neighborhood. Sometimes it seems that the resources for prevention, treatment, and cure of LBD are all in Houston taking care of cancer or some other more recognized disease. I long for the day when a convoy of resources brings hope to those who have lost their power because of LBD.

Thirteen years ago when Nelson was diagnosed, I would speak of his disease as Alzheimer's because no one knew what LBD was. Even many doctors and nurses had not heard of it. Now I call it what it is and try to educate each person, even if only to say it has features of both Alzheimer's and Parkinson's. On one of our errand days, Nelson's knees collapsed under him while we were walking into the office to get his eyes checked. A customer offered her assistance, and then after we had him in a wheelchair, she told me she was a nurse. I told her his diagnosis, expecting the usual blank response. She surprised me by saying she knew what it was. There *is* some progress.

Recently a friend returned to our church for a visit from Arizona where she and her husband had retired. She lost him three years ago to a diagnosis of "first Alzheimer's and then Parkinson's." As we talked, I suspected LBD and promised to send her a brochure. "It described him exactly," she wrote back to me.

The word is leaking out, but we need a flood. I now give brochures about LBD to everyone who has anything to do with Nelson's care. I don't have hope that the lights can ever come back on for Nelson. But I can work toward the day when our grandchildren, or perhaps even our children, can grow older knowing that they will not be stripped of their power by LBD.

My father died after a four-year battle with LBD. My mother is having such a hard time with guilt. She never fully accepted the disease and would sometimes be cruel with her words to him, out of anger, hurt, denial, and not fully understanding this horrible disease.

—Barbara

In what way has reading these caregiver stories changed your perceptions of dementia or caregiving in any way? Will your new awareness cause you to relate to families dealing with dementia in a different way? If so, what will change?

Before and after

September

Lewy body disease slices life into two: before LBD and after. Equal partnership evolves into caregiver and care receiver. Roles change into the managed and the manager. Companionable communication becomes silence. Old dreams become new realities. Old assumptions morph into new challenges.

We lived a pretty normal life until LBD symptoms began to prick our comfort. In our early years, we were good friends and we disdained those marriages where there was frequent quarreling. Sometimes Nelson and I would lock eyes in secret dismay at public displays of antagonism. We could usually talk things through when there was disagreement. We had our share of relationship conflicts, but they were the exception, not the rule.

When his unexplainable behaviors began to slide in alongside my changing menopausal body, I felt confused and unable to focus on why quarrels were becoming more frequent. Often these quarrels were brought on by trying to work together or by bungled communications. My refrain was, "It doesn't make any sense." I did not yet know that normal differences in tactics and communication had crossed the line into disease-driven dementia.

My increasing sensitivities to environmental fragrances and chemicals wore me down. The whiff of hairspray could send me into a severe reaction that would last for two weeks. "I get tired of your being sick," he said once. That was before LBD. Now it's my turn to weary at the restrictions of my spouse's chronic illness.

After life with symptoms began, the things we could orchestrate together melted away. While our siblings began to worry about our aging parents, I began to worry about Nelson. As time went on, siblings and peers began to follow their adult children and take retirement trips. We were trying to survive the onslaught of confusion over symptoms that in some respects were reflective of my eighty-year-old parents. I looked at Nelson's stooped posture one day and thought, "I am married to a man who seems as old as my father." We were in our early fifties.

Today my peers focus on being green, traveling, visiting children, and babysitting grandchildren. I focus on how to deal with another on the list of challenges of LBD and MCS (multiple chemical sensitivities). Is this another urinary tract infection or a move into incontinence? Is he taking Namenda needlessly? Is his TB test, required for daycare, up to date? Is having his eyes checked doable? How long would it take for him to decide each time the optometrist asks, "Is this clearer or this?" What is the next step for my own mental and emotional health? Can I find an in-home health aid who is fragrance free?

In 1997 when Nelson was first diagnosed with LBD, there was little to be read about the disease. What I could find said it was rare. Now we know that it's not rare, but is said to be the second leading cause of dementia and is frequently misdiagnosed.

Before diagnosis, when I would air my frustrations to peers about odd mishaps and behaviors, the response would often be "My husband is like that." Or empathizers would say, "It could happen to anyone." My intuition said this was different, but I couldn't seem to sort it out because, yes, very often he functioned in a way that seemed normal. Now I know that fluctuating cognition and function is part of the disease.

One morning, early in our marriage, we had the luxury of sleeping in. When the phone rang, Nelson got out of bed and took the framed marriage certificate off the wall. He then crawled back into bed, but never answered the phone. Puzzled, I asked why he did that.

"It might be Ed," he said, referring to his brother, but still not aware of what he had done. We shared that story and laughed with friends. Now I wonder, was this a first manifestation of the REM behavior disorder that often precedes other LBD symptoms, or was it just a fluke that really could happen to anyone?

When I first met Nelson, I was astonished at the smallness of his handwriting. It was miniscule, though for a time while he was teaching, it seemed to improve. Now I know that small handwriting is a symptom of the Parkinsonism and I wonder, could this have been a precursor?

Also, when I met Nelson I noticed something unique about the way he ran. His palms always faced behind him instead of facing his body. It looked stiff and awkward. Now I know that stiff movement is another way LBD manifests itself. Was this another small signal of what was to come or just a unique Nelson trait?

Before LBD I thought Nelson and I could make almost anything okay. Now, with LBD, he needs me to make everything okay for both of us. Some days I'm successful, other days not so much, but success and failure is part of all life, before or after LBD.

I am really struggling with future decisions. Some days the sadness just overwhelms every inch of me. My prayer every night is just for wisdom and strength.

—"Rhonda"

I am torn between the times he seems back and the times he goes away to that other place. Fifty-seven years of marriage keep us together, but it takes only minutes to lose him.

—Elizabeth Malm Clemens

If there has been an event in your life that dissected your life into before and after, what was it, and how has it made your life different or changed you?

What can he do today?

October

Adult daycare is a lifesaver and something I wouldn't want to be without. Sometimes, though, I want to tell the staff to leave me out of the equation. One morning Nelson told me that "tomorrow" he needed a costume. Tomorrow? Now how will that work, and what magic is going to make it happen? Me, I guessed.

Lucky for him, we had planned to be out and about that evening doing errands. Beyond stopping at the Salvation Army, I would make no promises. When we got there, I asked if he thought he could go into the store and look for something while I went across the street to buy printer paper. Of course, he said yes. What was I thinking? This is the man who still believes that he can do anything just by trying harder. As he went in the door and I drove away, the internal court began.

"You dropped him off to do this by himself? Do you remember how long it's been since he has done anything like this on his own?"

"So long I can't remember, but maybe...you never know. Anyway, I'll only be a minute."

"You'd better hope he's okay."

"I'll hurry."

"And what if something happens to you?"

"You're scaring me. I'll be really careful."

I did hurry, and back at the Salvation Army I found him wandering aimlessly around the store. I latched onto his hand and had him follow me around, looking for anything that might stimulate our imaginations. I'm not good at costuming. He, on the other hand, has always loved it.

I remember when, years ago, he came home wearing a rubber pullover mask of a wizened old man. He had on a trench coat, a hat pulled low over the life-like mask, and carried a cane. He came into the back yard where I was working and scared me witless as he immediately went into gales of laughter. Needless to say, it took me a little longer to laugh.

As we wandered through the Salvation Army, the only thing of interest was a black gaucho hat, so we went back to the car empty-handed. Then I had second thoughts. I asked Nelson if he could go back in and get the hat. I gave him money, and he went in while I waited in the car.

But the internal court went into session again.

"You're sending him in alone?"

"He was just there, and it's a straight walk to the back of the store where the hat is."

"What are you thinking?"

"I'm tired."

"He can't do it."

I gave up and went in. He was nowhere near the hat. I corralled him, took him to the hat, and, after trying it on, we took it to the checkout. The line was long, and I began to react to the fragrance dispensers used to mask odors. I was getting a headache. I showed Nelson where to stand in what appeared to be a motionless line and went outside, watching him through the storefront window. Periodically I stepped in to see if the line was growing shorter. It never seemed to be. Then I would go back out and wonder if he was going to tip over as I watched him lean farther and farther forward.

I studied the people in line. Could I give one of them the money and ask them to purchase it for us? He finally made it to the checkout, and I watched through the window as he handed over the money and took the change and his hat.

At home I pulled out a long, sleek, black raincoat of mine and tied the arms around his neck to look like a cape. I pressed the hat onto his head. Then I knew all we needed was a big silver duct tape "Z" on the front side of the hat and on the back side of the cape. He would be Zorro.

The next day Nelson left for daycare as Zorro, and came home as Zorro. What he did in between is limited only by the imagination. Zorro can do anything, right? Maybe, if nothing else, he got to believe that for a day he had no limitations. If so, it was worth the trouble.

He can barely speak anymore, even though he goes to speech therapy. I know he loves me dearly (as his daughter) and he knows I love him. It is just so difficult for me not to be able to hug him and make it all better. There is eternal hope, but in this life with Parkinson's disease and LBD, there is nothing to give my precious dad hope.

—Brenda De La Cruz

When have you been in conflict with yourself and your decisions? What do you do with that conflict? How do you resolve it?

Kaleidoscope

November

I receive emails from those who are in earlier stages of this journey with dementia. They bring to mind the kaleidoscope of my past and how my experiences have now shifted and changed to reveal patterns of life I never dreamed of. While some unseen hand turns the kaleidoscope, Nelson and I are beginning our forty-second year of marriage and still watching to see how the pieces of our lives will tumble into shapes and patterns of light and dark, hope and joy, grief and dismay.

"I let him drive," my Internet friend writes to me. It gives me pause. Was there actually a time when I "let" Nelson drive? I tug at the memories that seem so far away and realize that not only did I "let" him drive, there was an earlier life when we both assumed he would do all the driving. We liked it that way. I trusted his driving implicitly. He has, after all, driven city buses and taxi cabs while navigating the Chicago traffic. I can't recall ever feeling unsafe with his driving, that is, until LBD. That cataclysmic shift of the kaleidoscope changed everything and brings me back to the present.

The friend says she is going to have to start putting meds in an organizer. Was there a time when Nelson took his own meds without my prompting or help? My memory is foggy, but once upon a time I put them into the organizer, set each day's supply out, and by the end of the day, with maybe an occasional prompt, they would be gone. I pursue that memory further back through the fog to a time when Nelson never ever took medication for anything. He was never sick. He rarely had a cold and never missed a beat at work or play—until the kaleidoscope began to hint at something ominous.

The memories of our early life together are fading. You mean there was a time when I didn't have to help Nelson with eating, toileting, and dressing—a lifetime ago when he could actually help me with anything I asked him to do?

Since projects were outsourced long ago, now on many Saturdays we plan outings. Today he is clearly in no shape to take the outing we had planned. So I occupy myself at the computer while I wait for him to come to life. He is still in his nightclothes: white long johns turned backwards, a gray long-sleeved pullover top, and socks. When I finally hear him stirring, I propose a scaled-down version of our outing and ask if he is ready to get dressed to go. He says he is. I turn back to the computer and hear movement that indicates progress. Alas, when I turn to check on him, I find nothing has changed except that now he is wearing his shoes.

I am amused and fully aware that he is still not very functional, but there is no hurry to be out the door. I continue what I am doing at the computer for fifteen minutes or so and then give it another try, prompting, "If you want to go, you will need to get dressed." Again, I occupy myself for a time, then turn to see if he is ready to go. This time he has added his hat.

I have not always understood how people could say, "You have to laugh." Now I stare into that kaleidoscope and laugh at the ridiculous sight of my husband in his backward long johns, shoes, and hat—ready to go out the door and puzzled by my laughter. You have to laugh when you can. You have to let it be funny when you can. The kaleidoscope will shift soon enough to something that defies laughter. This time I laugh. And then I begin tugging and pulling at his clothes.

We go for a drive and have ice cream. There is no question: I drive.

The memory loss was well hidden for longer than any of us realized. He's now at home with our mother as caregiver. What's so odd about all this is that my dad can still teach Sunday school and lead a men's Bible study, but mostly doesn't know what day it is, still has some problem with incontinence, doesn't talk (as in carrying on a conversation), gives one or two word answers when asked a question, and can't make a decision about what to eat when we go out.

—"Iris"

Do you laugh as easily or as often as you would like? What keeps you from laughing at yourself or others? Do you have a laughing-at-myself story you can tell?

YEAR 13

"It's all right, questions, pain,
and stabbing anger can be poured out to the infinite One
and He will not be damaged.
Our wounded ragings will be lost in Him and we will be found.
For we beat on his chest from within the circle of His arms."
—Susan Lenzkes[6]

---

6. Susan Lenzkes, *When Life Takes What Matters: Devotions to Help You Through Crisis and Change* (Grand Rapids, MI: Discovery House Publishers, 1993), 32.

God, I thought you were standing by to keep us safe and happy.
Instead, I find you are too big for generalizations.
You are incomprehensible to my small mind.
You are indescribable with our puny words.
You are mystery.
Instead of trying to define, explain, understand,
let me yield to the mystery of you
who can't be
contained in words alone,
but need a universe, a galaxy,
a Spirit, and me for home.

—GHB

I have survived

January

In a month like the past one, I have to remind myself about all that I have survived.

Over the years I've learned there are many things I have to avoid to keep from having mild to severe reactions to my environment. The list is long and daunting, but I have managed the best I can by limiting where I go, what I do, and with whom I do it. Fragrance in anything from laundry detergent to hair coloring can trigger an allergic reaction with symptoms that can include burning sinus, headache, shortness of breath, muscle weakness, or a nose that drips like a faucet.

Caregiving is difficult by itself. When in a reaction, I have so much less to give. I've learned to be more open about my needs, which has been hard on some relationships, and challenges all of them.

On Thanksgiving I had a reaction that was the most severe I've had in years. That night I curled up in bed with chills, a headache, sinuses that burned like fire, and prickly sensations in my legs. I knew I was in trouble. The next day my daughter, who was visiting with her family from Kansas, thoughtfully suggested that we stay home rather than do the outings we had planned. She took care of meals and then brought out the games. Watching her family play games kept my mind off of how bad I felt lying there on the sofa sick and discouraged. This was *not* how I wanted it to be on those special visits from our daughter and family who live four states away. The next morning they were scheduled to leave and we said goodbyes.

Midweek I begin to realize that I was in no shape to deal with the weekend and full-time caregiving. I couldn't sleep. I had developed a tight cough and congestion and my voice was completely altered. I was using the prescription that I always had on hand, but I wasn't getting better.

I made some phone calls to get Nelson into respite care. I asked him if he would spend the weekend at a nearby facility, where our friend Glenna lived.

Glenna had been a babysitter for our children when they were young. We discovered that she was in a nearby care facility during a visit to share some of our hundreds of daffodils with residents. Nelson instantly recognized her bright smile and seemed drawn to her. He thought a long time before saying he could "probably pull it off."

That was ironic considering the lengths I have to go to each time he goes to respite. The Area Agency on Aging has to come out and do a home visit. Never mind that I am terribly sick and that bringing the fragrance of the caseworker into the house will increase my symptoms. The family physician has to fax his order for medications. I have to make arrangements with Nelson's daycare to take him to the care facility on Friday evening and pick him up there on Monday morning. I have to sign a dozen papers for the respite facility and pack his clothes. I told him, "You won't have to do anything. I will take care of it all."

The next evening after I reminded him of the plan, he stood bent over in the kitchen and spoke into the floor. With enough repetitions, I finally heard, "How are your bodily functions?" Somehow I knew what he was asking. I reassured him that I just needed a few days to regain my health. He cooperated fully in going.

Friday morning I sent him off. It seemed he actually was looking forward to going. He was more alert and articulate than he had been for a while. He asked if he could have a couple of dollars. I knew he was thinking of the candy machine that Glenna had treated him from. I rounded up all the quarters I could find and told him he had enough to get one thing each day. He would run out if he spent more than seventy-five cents a day, but I knew there was no use telling him that.

Monday morning, after three nights of little sleep, I was shaky and unable to think or focus. I knew I needed a doctor. I was stuck on which one would be most helpful. I broke into tears: "I need to do something but I don't know what."

That's when Sally knocked. I had called two days earlier to confess that I'd forgotten a walking date because I was sick. She chose this moment to show up unexpectedly at my door with groceries. Sally is a nurse and confirmed that I needed to see someone and helped me sort through my options. Just by showing up at precisely my lowest point, she helped me to believe that God is still somehow in this picture. The doctor gave me prescriptions for bronchitis and an infection.

Monday evening I was far from over the hump, but it was time for Nelson to come home. He walked in the door a different person. There was an odor. He hadn't had a shower the four days he was gone. He was unshaven. Half of the clothes I sent along were never worn. Wet clothes were in a bag along with his toothbrush and toothpaste. His eyes were glazed. There was a bruise from the ankle bracelet used for those who may wander. The quarters were all unspent. I mustered all my strength and gave him a shower, fed him, and put him to bed.

Soon another weekend with Nelson was staring me in the face. I still didn't feel well. On the phone my sister Micki said she and her husband, Roger, would be out for the weekend to help. They were scheduled to visit from out of state one weekend later for Christmas with extended family. I didn't want to ask this extra trip of them, but she insisted, reminding me that she has always said if I got sick she would come to help: "You have never cashed in."

The week that followed showed slow and small improvements. By the next weekend, when Micki and Roger came back, I was beginning to feel that the end of this episode was in sight. They would stay the week of Christmas. Christmas Day I went without an antihistamine for the first time since Thanksgiving and felt good. Then I began sneezing. By the next day my nose was dripping constantly, and I went back to the antihistamine unsure what had triggered this new onslaught. It was a long haul to health.

You have survived, I sometimes have to tell myself. You don't have to be any stronger than you are in this moment. Moments have stacked upon moments and you have survived. Survive only for this moment and you will be okay. Sometimes I can believe it.

I am always learning and finding the personal growth of compassion and strength that we find when we experience deep soul grief. An astute physio said your soul is torturing you with grief and that was a help to find my way through this to some degree.

—"Alice"

I am at the bottom of the barrel and just totally physically and mentally exhausted. Each day is worse than the other. I have a little help from caregivers. My daughter and I can hardly go any longer.

—Margarite

If you have experienced a time when you could only hope to make it one moment at a time, how did you get through it? If not, what has been the most difficult experience of your life, and how did you get through it?

Sometimes it matters

_____

March

Last summer on one of his more articulate days, "Good woman" was all he could get out. The inflection was assertive and commanding, but in good humor. He was ready for an outing, and his words meant, "Hurry up. I'm ready to go." He may not have been able to say exactly what he once would have, but I could translate. So it didn't matter.

I was the kid in grade school who hated history and the one in college who barely passed History of Civilization. I didn't want to memorize dates and read about dead people. In later years, I was the mom who hauled her kids to peace demonstrations. Reading about offensives, bazooka teams, foxholes, and generals never appealed to me.

But this winter, since Nelson likes history and I'm the reader, I decided it didn't matter: I read an historical account of the Battle of the Bulge to him.

We don't have a garage door opener. Whenever we are about to leave the house, Nelson pulls up the garage door, and I get into the car while he waits outside for me to back out. Then he pulls the door down before climbing into the car. This particular time he stood in the middle of the open door, directly behind the car, and waited for me to back out. When I didn't proceed, he became impatient. "Let's go!"

"I can't. You want me to run over you?" He looked at me blankly and grumbled without moving. I wanted it not to matter, but exasperation edged into my voice. "You have to get out of my way!"

Once he was in the car, I waited for him to fasten his seatbelt. His mistake had been exposed, and now he was determined to prove that he could do this task himself. I cut the car engine and waited, entertaining myself with impatient thoughts and practicing, "It doesn't matter." But he was struggling. "You want me to do it?" I finally asked hopefully.

"Yeah." His voice carried a muted anger and an infrequent acknowledgment that his mind had betrayed him.

I slipped the belt in place and had a brief sense of his loss at being stripped of so many coping skills. "You're a good man, Charlie Brown," I said trying to make it not matter for both of us.

"Yeah," he said, "and let that be a lesson to you."

"Let that be a lesson to me?" I retorted, poking fun at his response. I laughed because his annoyance at me regarding the garage door incident wasn't about me and didn't really matter. His eyes crinkled and he laughed. I was glad.

Managing his every mindless move, I get lots of practice telling myself it doesn't matter. He may lock the door when we are only stepping out to the yard. Or he may fail to lock it when we are leaving for the day. I find recyclables in the trash and trash in the recyclables. Anything that is round, from the sink to the toilet, is a receptacle for foil candy wrappers. Lights may be turned off when I'm in the room or left on in seldom-used rooms. He may push in my chair when I get up from the table, while his special, larger chair on wheels stands away from the table blocking the way. Or he may clear away the breakfast I haven't finished eating while his own empty dish is left on the table.

Practice . . . practice . . . practice.

I'm not a morning person so the less I have to do first thing, the better. I always set out the breakfast pills and dishes the night before. Then in the morning I thaw some frozen blueberries in the microwave to eat with my soymilk and cereal. Recently I had a restless night and got up for a few minutes hoping to work it off. Since I was up, I decided I could put the berries out and let them thaw in my bowl for a couple of hours. Wouldn't that be nice? There would be one less step in the morning.

But Nelson's mindlessness doesn't discern subtleties. I got up the next morning later than he did. Still groggy from lack of sleep, I came face-to-face with the kitchen in disarray. He had opened and mangled a cereal box that collapsed in my hand when I picked it up. Cereal was scattered here and there, and the place setting I had put out for him the night before was gone. My chair was pulled out. And my bowl—it was full of his cereal. My berries were covered with his cow's milk. Suddenly, it mattered.

Why?

Because caregivers give and give and learn to survive by saying it doesn't matter. We live with the mantra of "it doesn't matter." But we're human. We get slammed with moments of realization that we can't count on anything from this person. We have to buy a new toothbrush one too many times because ours wasn't hidden well enough. Or we are fighting our own tiredness or illness, and one more need, demand, or incapability breaks us.

Then when it does matter, when the loss, the loneliness, and the ludicrous send our equilibrium careening into impatience and exasperation, we have to remember to give ourselves the same monumental grace that we have been giving out. That is when it matters very much that we remember this: we matter, too.

My husband was a building engineer. Yesterday, our car broke down and he kept trying to mess with the engine while I was calling for help. I actually had to threaten him that I would scream bloody murder if he didn't stop. Even then, when my back was turned, he pulled the cap on the radiator without taking the proper precautions.

—"Mary Ann"

He would become angry if we discussed anything (anything that required problem solving). Many times he would take off in the car. He stopped going to church with me and began finding fault with everything. We did a remodel, and he micromanaged everyone. Yet he could not do a simple transaction at the bank. It's like he is two different people.

—Loretta Cortelyou

Do you think that you are able to have reasonable expectations of yourself and others? What expectations of yourself or others might you need to raise or lower? How good are you at giving yourself grace when you have not lived up to your expectations? Explain.

Bridging the gap

April

We all change over the years, and in any marriage the challenge is to grow together rather than apart. For those of us with a spouse who has Lewy body dementia (LBD), this undertaking is magnified and gradually becomes one-sided. Any sustained improvements to the relationship come from us. How we bridge the gap between our worlds becomes one more thing that morphs into our responsibility alone.

As Nelson moves further into LBD, he more easily loses his orientation to where he is and what is taking place. In the unfamiliar environment of vacation and air travel last month, it was evident that he missed his structure. I realized the toll it had taken on him. He sat next to me at a small table in an Atlanta airport sub shop where we waited for our next flight. Turning to me as if he were making polite conversation, he asked, "How many children do you have?" At home he frequently loses track of me, startling at my presence when I speak even though I am seated nearby. But he rarely loses track of who I am. These incidents keep me cognizant of the crevasse that memory loss has opened between us. I am overwhelmed by the leap it takes to cross it and sometimes ambivalent about whether I want to, because even if I manage to bridge the gap and create a connection, it will be unsustainable.

We have been home from vacation for one week. Nelson has been back in his routine and seems at ease, self-assured, cocky even. The man with a mission pokes his head in the bathroom door and wonders how I am doing. There is no doubt this is a reappearance of an old persona. The question is loaded. It means, "I'm ready to go to church and you should be ready to go too." As usual, he fails to have a concept of time. It's forty minutes until church begins and a ten minute drive to get there.

Rather than annoy him with the reminder that he wants to go too early, I tell him I'm doing okay. I'm feeling lucky. Maybe he will accept this, sit down in his chair, and fall asleep. Instead he comes back with, "I'll pull the car up."

Alarms go off and adrenalin surges. He hasn't driven the car in something like thirteen years so I tell him emphatically that he will not! I give him the benefit of the doubt, saying, "Do you mean you'll pull the garage door up? You can do that!" He disappears, and I feel relieved that I seem to have averted a confrontation.

Later, when I'm ready to go, I reach into the key basket beside the door and the keys are not there. Did I leave them in my coat pocket? He's busily standing in my way trying to usher me out the door, which I cannot open because he is in front of it. When I tell him that I don't know where the keys are, he reaches into his pocket, pulls them out, and nonchalantly hands them over.

The adrenalin isn't completely out of my system as I pave the road to church with consternation. Ever since I began doing all the driving, he habitually points his finger at crossings to tell me it is safe to go even though he is only checking from his direction. I ignore the "help." Some primitive animal in me wants to sit at each intersection a while longer than necessary to prove that I will go when I am ready, but I ignore that too, choosing not to widen the gap that is always there between our worlds, ready to swallow us.

Later in the day, we walk in the park. Afterwards, as we prepare to leave, Nelson scoots into the driver's seat. The keys are safely in my pocket, so I watch this new phenomenon to see if he's going to realize what he's done, but he doesn't. When I question him, he says he's going to "follow them," indicating the car of my sister and her husband who are beginning to pull out of the lot. It's not until I tell him he can't drive that he realizes his mistake. Then he offers no resistance and heavily pulls himself out from behind the wheel and moves to the passenger side. I decide his comfort at being home from vacation and in familiar surroundings has taken over his muscle memory and without the aid of cognition has taken him back to old times. For some reason these sorts of guesses and explanations help me cope with the ever-widening gap.

There are times when Nelson needs to prove to one of us that he can conquer something. This often manifests itself with the seatbelt in the car. When one too many things have defied his abilities, he'll get into the car and try to fasten the belt himself. "I almost have it," he will say as I watch him try to force the end into an illusive slot. He dodges unruly lumps of a winter jacket and persists, oblivious to the passage of time. Sometimes he gets it and is triumphant. Other times one of us gets exasperated and he accepts my help. When I can identify with his helplessness and loss, the gap closes a little. When all I can see is *my* loss, the gap pulls me in and for a time consumes me. Then I have to once again open my heart to the anointing process of grief, its expression, and letting go.

Occasionally, when I'm helping Nelson with a simple task of dressing or toileting, he becomes aware that something he's doing isn't working. Without the tools to communicate, he is embarrassed and goes into spasms of giggles. When I am able to scrap the importance of the task and giggle and laugh along (even though I may not know what we're laughing about), the moment brings us together in his world, rather than chipping away at the fragile bridge between us.

The communication gap sprinkles into all of life. When I try to make sense out of words I can't hear and phrases that won't connect as he labors on in hope for understanding, then the gap becomes a chasm, the losses flood over me, and my body becomes heavy with the sadness of it all.

On rare occasions and at the most unexpected times, I get glimpses of the Nelson I fell in love with, and then he is the one who bridges the gap between our worlds. One day, he was restless, moving around the living room looking for his shoes. But his shoes were right there in plain sight. I pointed this out, but he continued to search, stopping to block my view of the TV. I protested with telltale exasperation in my voice and again asked what he was looking for. He repeated the same indistinguishable answer and lumbered away. I stared at the TV feeling frustrated at the gap and defeated by my scolding voice. After roaming a bit longer, Nelson bent down to my face and, with a rare and poignant clarity, he enunciated clearly, "Goodnight, wild woman." Then with a grin, he added, "I think I love you." With that he turned to climb the stairs to bed. My heart melted and for a brief and glorious moment our worlds spun as one.

It's Saturday night, the end of my biggest caregiving day; he is tucked into bed and ready to sleep. He didn't have much energy for the walk at the park; his knees buckled when he went to pick up the mail at the end of our drive; his hands failed to cooperate when we ate lunch; he was too tired to do anything but sit in the car at the grocery store; and his efforts at communication often got no more from me than "I can't understand you." Yet, he thanks me for a good day. That is the Nelson that astounds me: his high tolerance for what to me looks so intolerable. For that now, I count my blessings and know that we have somehow been successful in keeping a bridge intact to each other's worlds for yet another day.

Our son is getting married and I just can't seem to feel the happiness I should. I actually am dreading the day. How are we going to share the happiness? How am I going to manage [my husband]? Hopefully he will have a good day. It's the old "rollercoaster syndrome." He seems to be regressing since his fall.

—Rita McAdam

Now come on. We struggled in our marriage since I married him at seventeen, twenty-nine years ago. Then the struggle of the disease for eleven years. And all I could see for the fifteen days in watching him leave this life was what a sweet man. He was a baby boy to me. Thank you, Jesus, for his new brain and body.

—Katherine Holder

Try to think of a time when you felt that there was a fragile bridge between you and another person. How much effort did you give to bridging the gap? Did the relationship survive? If your spouse were diagnosed with dementia, how much effort do you see yourself giving to bridging the gap?

What can I do?

June

When I received an email from a longtime friend who wanted to know what she might do to help a caregiver in her family, I had flashbacks of the early days, before diagnosis, when so much of what Nelson did was not making sense. We would meet someone who would ask how we were doing and Nelson would say, "Fine," and then talk about teaching as if he still were, even though he was on sick leave. Perhaps his lack of awareness combined with denial kept him reflecting life as he wanted it to be. In any case, it didn't reflect the truth of the matter for me. I would stand by silently, without words, knowing we were not fine, but feeling powerless and alone. So friends or family would walk away with no clue about our reality.

Until then in our marriage, I enjoyed letting Nelson be the spokesperson in social situations. But now I was dismayed by his misrepresentation of our circumstances and alarmed at how lost I felt because of it. I needed to find my voice. I needed people who knew about our search for answers to ask me privately, "How is Nelson?"

We have always enjoyed togetherness in our marriage. But now I needed to separate myself in order to give voice to my confusion and to the puzzling things that were happening. When people approached me privately and asked how Nelson was doing, I had the opportunity I needed. Those conversations helped me begin to accept my new reality and initiate the numerous changes that a caregiver has to make in order to move into a new, difficult, and unfamiliar role.

Family members and others who wanted to be supportive were helpful just by taking the initiative to connect while giving lots of grace when I was not responsive, or lots of empathy when I needed to express frustration, fear, or grief.

To complicate adjustment, we caregivers may have all kinds of previously unrecognized, dormant, unhelpful beliefs to confront and sort through:

A loving spouse should never be impatient with their partner who can't be held accountable for his actions.

A person with faith wouldn't question God or feel angry about loss.

A caring spouse should always be there for the diagnosed no matter what the cost to themselves.

It's weak to need help.

I'm on my own.

Dementia is humiliating.

I found myself struggling with all of these beliefs at one time or another. Lost in a maze of confusing events and unable to live up to my own expectations for acceptance, I would then feel guilty. I needed people who could listen, validate the pain of loss, and support the transition to more helpful beliefs.

Today the question I need to hear has shifted to "How are you doing as a caregiver?" This question from an empathetic listener helps me continue to process my reality. It is a difficult question to ask because it invites the sharing of pain and requires the listener to share some of the feelings of helplessness. But when someone can ask, listen, and simply hold the ache of it with me, the emotional heaviness dissipates.

I have found my voice. When I want others to help me problem solve, I tell them that I want help. More often, I want them to listen with reflective prompts that help me probe my own emotional workings. I have also learned to say, "I don't want to problem solve right now." For me, the stress of the relentless goodbye has required enormous amounts of talking through the emotions. Those who listen and affirm have helped me regain my equilibrium by validating the struggle.

I truly believe the people who walk beside me—whether listening, problem solving, or helping in chores or caregiving—have given Nelson the quality of life he has because it is their support that has helped me find my way one day at a time. It's not only the child who needs a village. People with dementia and their caregivers need a village, too.

So, villagers, what can you do? Ask about the cared for, but don't stop there. Ask about the caregiver. Ask if the caregiver wants your help in problem solving. Ask if the caregiver just needs to talk. Listen to the struggles for acceptance. Listen to the faith doubts without platitudes or judgments. Ask how you can be a part of the village and then validate the strength and the struggle of caregiving. That's what you can do.

I'm quietly living the life he is, only I'm trying to do it alone, and it's getting so difficult. I feel I am going to lose my mind before he loses his.

—"Beverly"

My mother and I live in different states. Where I used to call her twice a week, I now call her every day or every other day. I understand that where she used to have my dad to converse with, she no longer has him. I've long said to Mom, "I'm not worried about Dad. Dad is content and relatively happy. I'm worried about you."

—Donna Reinbolt

What are your beliefs about how you and others should be in the world? Do you think your beliefs would hold up in a relationship that includes dementia? How hard would it be for you to change those beliefs to accommodate a spouse or parent with dementia?

Another go at freedom

July

Sometimes, when I'm pushed to the limit, I will assault the page so that I don't direct my exasperation at Nelson. This is one of those times.

He has been more physically active lately, on the prowl instead of just sleeping in his chair. He's pulling things from the closets, taking books from the shelves, and looking for something he can't name. He throws messy trash into the recycle bin, leaves lights on and water running, and moves my clothes around. My favorite paring knife disappears; a half shelf of flower pots and vases lie broken on the garage floor. My sense of order is repeatedly overthrown. I go behind him to search and restore until the proverbial straw breaks me. Yesterday it happened not once, but twice.

Now, this morning he saved half of the last banana for me. He thought of me and planned ahead? It is almost more than I can believe. It was going to be my breakfast since he didn't seem interested in bananas lately. I know that counting on anything is risky, but it's hard not to fall into the expectation trap once in a while. I tell him, "Thank you for saving some of the banana for me." But then I wonder why my heart just doesn't feel the gratitude. I should be ecstatic, shouldn't I?

Recently, his pattern has been to fall into a dead sleep when he gets home from adult daycare and then become active at bedtime. One night I tried walking him around early in the evening to keep him awake, but it was like leading a statue. I tried putting his hands on my shoulders with him walking behind. Soon I was carrying dead weight. I told him he was too heavy. He eased up on the pressure, but I knew it couldn't last. Now I let him sleep for a couple of hours upon coming home and then feed him later. His eyes stay closed as he eats, and I often have to hold his head up to get the food in his mouth without it falling off the spoon. He manages to eat in some gray state between awake and asleep.

Nelson's sporadic second wind, though, is the problem. Last night about 9:30, when I was ready to head for bed, he started rummaging in the kitchen for something to eat. He wanted food and something else that I couldn't discern. I only wanted to go to bed.

Finally, he uttered the word "rope" and started down the basement steps—not the direction I wanted to go, and I didn't know what kind of rope we were looking for or why. Trying to get that information could send us both over the edge. I waited, hoping he would come back up and let me lead him to bed. Instead, he gave a sharp whistle to let me know that he wanted me to help him find the rope. I called back,

"I'm not a dog and I'm not coming down there. It's bedtime." I went crashing over the edge. I slammed the door and a few other things, let words fly, and then stomped upstairs to bed. When he came up, I asked if the lights were all turned off. He said they were. I went down the first flight of stairs and peered down the second. They were not. I went down and turned them off. Then I climbed back up the two flights to bed.

In one of Nelson's more cognizant moments, he wondered how people at church might feel about our "popping in whenever we feel like it." I'm in survival mode here trying to keep myself healthy while dealing with two ridiculously isolating and difficult "his and her" diseases, and he is worried about what people think? I feel pushed to the edge again and heavy with feelings, judgments, and consternation. He lives in a fantasy world with no LBD or chemical sensitivities. Can he truly not remember? Our friend Chip, who recently passed away from LBD talked about his disease and acknowledged its effects. I reason that Nelson's optimistic nature seems to cross the line into denial. If you don't acknowledge it, it isn't there. It's an extravagance I can't afford.

When he was finally in bed tonight, we observed our ritual. I asked if he was all set. He said he was. Then we kissed goodnight and he said, "Goodnight darling." In the quiet softness of the night light, only I am left with all of the memories of my disintegration and dissatisfaction.

I think about the bird that got tangled in my garden net, how, after twenty minutes of cutting it away thread by thread, I held it in my palm gently and then opened my hand, releasing it to freedom. I want to snip away the indignant threads that wrap around my insides so that I, too, can be free. And so I write until one by one I've acknowledged the defeat, disappointment, and discouragement and given them over to the healing power of grief and grace. I want to live the exhilaration of the bird flying into another go at freedom.

He is now in the veterans home. It breaks my heart and it is so empty here, but I just could not manage any longer. He seems to be adjusting well and gets such good care. I just cry all the time.

—Margarite

We had no idea why Mom would go on these missions to find things and want to feed people. According to her, our house was full of people. Everything she has done, I have read about in your stories. I thought the hallucinations and voices were from the meds.

—Cheri Kjersem

Is it difficult for you to acknowledge defeat, disappointment, or discouragement? Why or why not? In what circumstance have you experienced the "healing power of grief and grace"?

It is time

———————

August

I've asked myself many times how I will know when it's time for me to consider long-term care for Nelson.

Thinking about it, my heart would always resist and say that I can do this one more day. Gradually I have come to realize that my heart will always say no, but it's time to listen to the voice in my head that is saying it is time. My inner resources are drained and dry. I seem to have lost any sense of well-being. Discouragement and depression hover. "One more day" isn't working anymore and my aching body is telling me it is time.

I have watched Nelson go from an intelligent, self-sufficient, entertaining, and engaging person to a dependent, unresponsive, illusive shadow of who he was. In the meantime I have aged from fifty feeling forty to sixty-four and feeling old and spent.

In the evening I lead him around by both hands to get him ready for bed. He does a slow shuffle as if he is afraid to take a step. My physical strength is declining, and I find myself wondering more often if I'm going to have to call for someone to help get him up the stairs to bed or out of his chair.

At night I hear Nelson on his way to the bathroom. I lie there resisting awakening and wait to see if he will make it back to bed without help. Sometimes he does. Other times the silence is too long, and I get up to find him stuck in some frozen stance, or attempting to clean up a spill, or unable to remember how to turn off the water.

That happened while I was visiting our daughter out of state. My sister Micki, who was staying with Nelson, found him in the middle of the night, the sink stopper closed, the water running and overflowing onto the bathroom floor. "We need a plumber," Nelson said. "Call Derrick." Then he opened the cabinet under the sink, reached in, and turned off the supply line like our plumber friend Derrick might do in an emergency. One can only wonder.

Sometimes he has a nightmare and wakes me with frightened noises, or he falls out of bed. I awake abruptly, adrenaline pumping. Then sleep comes slowly and eats away the night. My body is losing its resilience. I'm tired.

It takes my total focus when he's trying to communicate. I wait long minutes for him to get words out and pay close attention trying to understand, but most often the words are too quiet and garbled. After I tell him I can't understand, I feel such an emptiness and loss for us both. And then I distance myself from him to avoid the hurt. It's like I'm trying to maintain a relationship with a person who is never home when I visit.

I want to tell him about something that has given me a rare feeling of animation. He is unresponsive. The animation fizzles like a dud firecracker. I go back to living the life of disconnect.

"My patience is gone," I tell a friend. "I have none for anybody or anything."

"It's the caregiving," she says.

My stamina has crumbled. I can no longer give the care he deserves. That's humbling.

"You have done it longer than most people would have," people assure me.

Another says, "Don't wait too long. My neighbor did and was almost over the edge." It's not hard for me to imagine that.

So, overruling the heart that will always say no, I have begun to prepare us both for his long-term care.

This morning he needs help gathering the "posies" from my flower beds that will go along to the daycare staff. We go from flower to flower, adding some delicate lacy fennel to brown-eyed susans and then some purple larkspur. He holds the vase in his hand. I cut the flowers and arrange them in the vase. I have just placed the last flower when he says, "I think about you a lot during study period." My heart melts into a very warm puddle that collects in the hard shell of my reality. I put my arm around his waist, and we walk together in a rare moment of connection and found fondness.

After the bus picks him up, I come in to eat breakfast at the table where a small bouquet is long past needing replacement. It's time for our table to have a fresh bouquet as well.

It's time for me to give what I can—the night disruptions, the feeding, the tugging and pulling of clothes, the cleaning up after—to someone else.

It's time for me to be with him in a place where I am the anticipated guest, where the caregiving doesn't constantly interrupt my sense of wellness. It's time for me to recover the fondness for him that eludes me under the losses, aches, and strain of at-home caregiving.

I return to the garden and lose myself in the flowers, picking a small bouquet. Inside, I place them in the center of the table. It is time.

I made up a little saying that I use to remind myself that "there are a lot of people in nursing homes, and they're not there because people don't love them. They're there because people have limits."

—Florrie Munat

At some point we are going to have to place "Pap," but I am hoping God takes him while he is with us. He has end-stage cardiac disease, and two years ago his MDs told us he would not last three months. It is as if the LBD has "cured" his cardiac problems.

—"Lucy"

In what situation have your heart and your head disagreed? How did you resolve it? How do you think you would handle putting a spouse into a long-term care facility? If you have ever had conversations with a spouse or parent about options for care, how did it go? When do you think would be the best time for those conversations?

A caregiver's prayer

September

We stand at the window of our front door watching the morning fog lie like a thick, wet blanket over the damp landscape. On the horizon, the early sun sends fingers of light that shift and move, filtering through the breaking fog like a giant kaleidoscope in slow motion. The black silhouette of a tree stands tall and proud in its misty shawl. With each passing moment, streams of light penetrate the fog at yet higher angles, shifting the picture as if to announce new possibilities. Nothing stays the same, it tells me—not the achingly beautiful life of love, not the dark journey of sorrow.

We wait for Nelson's adult daycare bus, for the sun to warm us, and for the day to unfold. What will it bring? I've placed his name on three waiting lists for long-term care. The first choice facility has five people ahead of him. I am ready. The decision seems right, and now that it is made I hope for things to move quickly. I've talked with him about it, but he has forgotten.

I will continue to talk with him at appropriate times—not too often, because he becomes full of questions and worries that he can't articulate, exasperating us both. But neither do I want him to feel blindsided.

The bus arrives as the sun continues to burn off the moisture that has cluttered the misty air like a visual static. The heat begins to soak my joints with welcome warmth, an invitation to action. It begins to dry yesterday's laundry still on the line: a reminder of unfinished business.

Questions crowd my mind. How will we adjust? Will I be able to visit his new environment and manage my reactivity to fragrances and cleaners? How long will we wait? I know the fears I bring to this day and the changes that lie ahead. Or do I? Let me find wisdom and courage as predictable as daylight. Burn off the haze that keeps me from seeing clearly. Remove the static that keeps me confused and questioning.

What will I find today under this ever-brightening ribbon of sunlight? Let me listen to our voices, God, yours and mine, comingling as they sift through need and want, fear and reassurance, loss and loneliness, gifts and gratefulness. Let our conversations inform my course in choosing, speaking, and acting. Without attentiveness to your words and mine, I'm lost and helpless to penetrate the fog of change. Let me wrap each change, whether it brings love or sorrow, in a ribbon of summer sun boldness and receive each shift in my life with anticipation for its potential to paint new pictures, giving birth to renewed hope.

I miss my husband's companionship and the help
he always provided in decision making. I go to
church every Sunday and spend the time praying for
patience and understanding and spiritual help in my
caregiving.

—Helen Blomstrom

My husband is now in memory support. We just
celebrated our fifty-fourth wedding anniversary
there. Yet I am only seventy-four. Who am I now?
Better yet, who do I want to become?

—Joy Golliver

Why do you think it's important to the author to
include her own voice in the listening to God? How
aware are you of your own needs, wants, losses,
fears, and loneliness? Do you voice them? If you do,
how is that helpful? If you don't voice them, why
not?

Three times a lady

_____

October

Thirty-some years ago, Nelson kissed me goodbye and went off to school to teach a room full of active fifth graders. Before he left, he told me to be sure to listen to the local radio station at ten that morning. I went about my morning chores, as was my habit, listening to National Public Radio or perhaps the stereo. A couple of minutes before ten, I went to the radio and dialed back and forth trying to find Skip Hornyak's familiar voice at 1480 WHBC. To my dismay, I couldn't find it. I knew the DJ's voice, but what else was I listening for? After some time searching, I gave up.

That night, Nelson came home and asked me if I had heard his request on the radio. I had to admit that I hadn't. He had requested that the Commodores' "Three Times a Lady" be played for our wedding anniversary ("You're once, twice, three times a lady, and I love you") and I had missed it. How could I have let this brief jaunt into the romantic get away? Later, when I heard the song for the first time, my regrets grew.

After that, I would be out shopping or driving the car, and when that song came on I would feel both instant regret and a heart full of gratitude for the little romantic splurge Nelson took that day. Eventually I went out and bought the CD.

When we celebrated our thirty-eighth anniversary, my sister helped Nelson buy a card for me. He was eight years into his LBD diagnosis and seemed only to know that he was supposed to give it to me. He didn't know that he was giving it a day early and had nothing to say when he gave it. The next day on our anniversary I decided to create a little celebration by putting on "Three Times a Lady":

> Thanks for the times that you've given me;
> The memories are all in my mind.
> And now that we've come to the end of our rainbow,
> There's something I must say out loud.

I heard the irony in the words, "The memories are all in my mind." I had seen those memories slipping away from him. Who could have guessed that at the end of our rainbow we would be untangling LBD mysteries instead of exploring retirement's pot of gold? I found myself acutely missing the Nelson of the past and needed to grieve again the loss of hope that the partner Nelson had been could ever return.

That thirty-eighth year I knew he would not be able to do as we had done in the past—stand with our arms around each other, moving slowly to the music. This time we could only stand and hold each other, he leaning more and more on me. Then he had to sit down. I told myself that the song expressed his sentiment whether he could express it or not. I felt tenderness for his helplessness and sadness for my loneliness.

A lot of anniversary years have come and gone since then. Some have been celebrated, some barely acknowledged. Now we have just remembered our forty-third. I had decided not even to mention it, to avoid the bitter sweetness of it. He, in a startling moment of recall, reminded me.

So we listened to some favorite music: Neil Diamond, Eric Clapton, and then I put on the Commodores for our traditional "Three Times a Lady." I told Nelson he didn't get to sit this one out, and we did a "one-two-three" pull up from his chair, my weight barely giving me the leverage I needed to lift him. We stood with our arms around each other while his body, stiff with LBD, moved very little and his feet not at all. His head got heavier on my shoulder, and his chin dug in sharply. Then I was propelled abruptly across the room as his feet broke out of their frozen stance. By then I had had enough, and he needed to sit down.

Now the efforts to redeem the romance that once existed in what seems like another lifetime must be discarded like some silly fantasy. Once I was three times a lady, and he was known to call himself Don Quixote. When I put him to bed last night, I asked him if I'm still three times a lady. A smile spread across his face, and, in spite of a day when my patience had come up short, he said, "Maybe four."

It's painful, it's draining, and it's not fair. Yesterday was our twenty-seventh wedding anniversary, and I spent the day reminding him of who I was and why I was here. He asked me if I was getting paid to be here, and I told him, "There isn't enough money to pay me for being here with you." I meant it as a statement of love—the hidden message was for me to know.

—"Frances"

What special traditions or celebrations would have to change in your marriage if a spouse had middle-to late-stage dementia? How would that change your feelings about that tradition or celebration?

No bed in long-term care

December

I have chosen a facility that would seem to best meet Nelson's need for long-term care. But like Mary and Joseph, I find there is no room.

Sometime before 2003, when both my parents were in a nursing home, I began to acknowledge that I might some day need long term care for Nelson. I was told it would be good to get his name on a list so that when the time came there would be no waiting. At the time, this need still seemed so remote that I submitted his name with relative ease to the same facility my parents were in. Then we went on with the perplexing task of adjusting to LBD. Time eventually took both my parents. I brought help into our home a few hours each week to assist with Nelson. Years went by and I never heard from the nursing home, but it was forty miles away. By this time I had begun to explore closer facilities.

Occasionally I would take a respite weekend, and Nelson would stay in a nursing home for a few days. In this way we experienced different facilities firsthand and learned what kind of care he might get. I soon discovered that some of the places that give the best care were private pay only, and once Nelson went on Medicaid, those places would have to be dropped as options. Thus began the trying process of finding long-term care.

More than a year ago, a facility with an excellent reputation came to my attention. I inquired about Medicaid, and they said they accept it. Its location was reasonably close to where we live. We were invited to eat a meal there. This family-owned facility seemed to be attentive to clients, and the two dogs that roamed the halls added interest for Nelson who had always liked dogs. I felt satisfied that this was my first choice. I put his name on a waiting list. More than a year went by, but I had not heard from them. I called to inquire about where we were on the list. They said, "You need a Plan B."

Not all facilities will provide respite care, but I began to use respite weekends more often to explore the facilities that did. The facility that sent him home with a scar from the leg monitor was immediately crossed off the list.

In one facility, I stayed an hour or so before leaving him there for the weekend. This facility looked very inviting in a previous tour. But that first hour before I left him told me otherwise. During that time, an unanswered buzzer at the nurse's station and a freezing cold dining room told me this was not where I wanted him to be either. This facility also lost his clothes during his two-day stay, and I had to make several trips before I'd finally retrieved them all.

I began looking at facilities farther away. At the recommendation of a neighbor, I found a place twelve miles from home. I visited, talked to the spouse of a resident, and got excited. This seemed like the ideal place. It became my new first choice. After putting his name on a waiting list and calling several times to see where we stood, I again heard the dreadful words, "You need a Plan B."

"You *are* Plan B," I told them.

I have now put his name on another list as Plan C. This facility doesn't do respite care, but several people have recommended it. It is twelve miles of city driving from our house. It is an older facility and has more of an institutional look, so it remains my third choice. I have learned that once a person has been admitted to the skilled nursing unit, that person has priority for a bed when it becomes available in the dementia unit. Someone on the list who is outside the facility must wait. Nelson's physical health is good, so there is nothing in sight that might admit him through that route.

In the meantime, the messages are coming in from caregivers and friends. A friend reports, "He was pretty lost today at church."

A note in our caregivers' notebook from my sister, who provides morning respite care and then takes him to adult daycare, says, "Nelson barely able to do anything this a.m. Seems unable to wake up. Not sure if we'll make it out of here!"

And from his adult daycare, "He was uncharacteristically confused today."

Nelson's knees have recently started buckling at unexpected times. He started to go down outside the grocery store, and I stood there for a long moment, trying to hold him up until someone stopped to help. At home in the evening, he is unable to move his feet more than an inch or two at a time, and he needs pushing and pulling to keep going. Yet true to LBD unpredictability, during a recent daytime walk he took off at a brisk pace so that we were nearly running to keep up with him.

Last week, the Plan C facility said a room could be available in a few weeks. The Plan B facility also called to ask if we still want to be on the list and, if so, did we want something soon? When I said yes, both trepidation and hope somersaulted inside me. It's time, but coming face to face with the possibility of this change stirs up fears.

And so in this season of Advent, I wait for a bed. Will it be in the inn of choice, or will I have to make do with some lowly stable? I wonder about the meeting of the human and the divine. Isn't all of life lived in Advent—waiting, watching, longing for that meeting with God—when human entanglements and securities are exposed to the light of divine truth and we know that whatever comes we will be loved and find our way?

Year after year I've watched the Nelson I married drift further from me. Sometimes platitudes of faith have washed up, faded and meaningless. Now during this Advent season, my thoughts have percolated and coalesced into a poem that expresses my journey, my advent.

Advent
Birth to death
Living
Between the crush
Of human fear
And God's divine presence
Watchful
For God's intersection
Into today
Longing for more
Than the illusion
Of safety and security
Waiting for faith
That is not dependent on what is seen
And comfort
That is not dependent on what is held
Submitting human ego aspirations
To the Divine
Then unwittingly
Grasping again for control
Letting
The life journey
Shed light
On the God within
Lifetime learning
To trust in each unknown
That God has already come

God infused
Into the squeeze
Between human fear
And the tentative hope of lagging faith
All of life
In Advent

Have you ever felt that "platitudes of faith washed up faded and meaningless," and would you admit it if you did? Why or why not? What helped or hindered your faith in those circumstances? Which part of the Advent poem do you identify with most?

YEAR 14

Telling your story is not to cause you pain. . .
someone needs to be with you in the pain for you to heal.
—Keith Ablow[7]

---

7. From a television interview, used with permission of Dr. Ablow.

I receive the gift of you
in whatever form that comes.
If suffering, then let me suffer with grace.
If abundance in mercy, then let me be merciful.
If you can enter this human condition,
Let me open the door and not dictate to you
how you will be with me.

—GHB

Waiting

January

I woke up this morning and thought how a decade and a half of my life has gone by watching Lewy body dementia (LBD) do its relentless, debilitating work. Like the autumn tree letting go of one leaf at a time, I have watched things I once took for granted drift down into a pile of loss at my feet.

First, it was letting go of the teacher coming home with a briefcase and paycheck. Then it was the competent and assured driver who navigated us safely through any kind of traffic or weather. The partner who could do anything—from fixing the car to helping me find the mistake in the checkbook—disappeared. The articulate, funny stories that entertained and helped me to lighten up—fallen by the wayside, along with the camaraderie of communication that kept our relationship alive, safe, and growing.

Finally, I had to surrender the right to have any expectations of him. Those expectations could now only keep us apart and breed disappointment. So they have fluttered to the ground with everything else.

With both Nelson's disease and my extreme allergic reactions, over and over I have had to let go of what I thought was reasonable to expect or believe. Many times I have felt stripped and empty and wondered, what now? What do I believe? What do I trust? What do I hope for? I have watched sunrise and sunset, waiting for answers and hope.

Answers are basic and few. God is somewhere in this picture. I get vignettes of that truth from nature, from the people who have reached out to me, from other stories of struggle and pain.

Hope is illusive but comes in moments of grace that are unpredictable and unplanned. It comes in an evening sunset that spreads its blanket of color over the earth and melts the gray winter landscape. It comes from a few simple words spoken by one who cares, or from hearing someone else's story of struggle and faith.

A new kind of faith is emerging. It has more questions than answers. This faith I am in has much longing. It holds those longings in sacred trust with God, has few expectations and contains a mustard seed of hope. It does much listening for God and much waiting for the movement of God. It is a faith of waiting. I wait for God to show me in the whole of my story that the mystery of faith is not in vain.

I haven't been able to embrace the beauty of waiting.
Waiting has brought disappointment—as in, we'll
travel when Don retires or Don and I will have
time together when Mother is gone or Don will be
happier when football season comes.

—"Beth"

Think about a time when you felt "stripped and
empty." What were the circumstances and how did
it affect your beliefs and faith? How would you
describe your faith today? How is it different or the
same as it was ten or twenty years ago?

Longing to be known

February

It's the bottom-of-the-barrel time of year. The cold, gray days and long evenings stretch ahead. Keeping in good health is hardest during these long winter months. On some days outdoor walks are impossible, and gradually my body succumbs to stiffness, new aches, chronic sinusitis, and general fatigue. I'm scraping the bottom of the barrel for something to keep me going.

In a chance encounter, an acquaintance says, "I'm praying for you." I grope for words that will reflect the sense of what I feel. Is it defeat? Is it acceptance? Is it cynicism or numbness? I'm not sure. I say, "Thank you." I've truly appreciated the countless people who have volunteered their prayers for us over the years. But this time I want more, though I can't say what. Her words that were meant to encourage fall outside of me.

Lots of people pray for me. But the prayers don't get me what I want: the companionship of the husband who knew me better than anyone else. The prayers don't bring back the knowing wink or the eyes that lock with mine in some secret nonverbal exchange. He no longer knows my likes and dislikes, what excites or bores me. Now he may turn his head to the wrong side to find my voice. Sometimes his eyes are glazed and I can see no sign of recognition.

The prayers don't get me that easy exchange of conversation with Nelson that my hungry memory calls up from long ago. Now, often the words are soundless puffs of air moving across his lips. He believes he is communicating. I don't have the heart to say "I can't understand you" one more time. I say "Hmm" and turn on the TV for another evening of hollow company.

The prayers don't bring back the person who would remove a splinter from my dominant hand, rub out a tight muscle in my shoulder, open a stubborn jar, find my lost book, reach a high shelf, keep track of car maintenance, or lend a hand in our adult children's remodeling projects.

That should-have-been life is now a distant memory. Instead, I continue to interpret sounds for him, shadow him, rescue him, feed him, dress him, entertain him, manage life for him, and mold my life to his needs.

And I read. Right now it's nonfiction only. Memoirs drop me for a time into the aches and traumas of someone else's life. Someone else's resilience reaches up from the page and shores up my crumbling resolve. They have survived. I can, too. Or, when I have lost God in my story, he shows up in someone else's. There my vision is not so clouded. It fosters belief that I can find him in mine.

It happened as I read *Shattered Silence* by Melissa G. Moore. As a fifteen-year-old girl, she was doing her very best to survive. Then she was raped, resulting in pregnancy. Her home life was a shambles. Her father, a serial killer, was in prison. She writes:

> When I realized I was contemplating the end of my life, I snapped out of it . . . only long enough to pray to the God who was such a mystery to me.
>
> Dear God, please help me, I have nowhere to turn except to you. If you know who I am, if I'm supposed to be here for any reason, please let me know.
>
> Exhausted I fell back to sleep. When I awoke, I felt like I had been in the most delicious dream. It was filled with so much joy—like I had never known before. I felt peace and comfort and the most amazing, unconditional love I had ever experienced. I reveled in the feeling, half awake, half asleep. When I finally woke fully, still in my darkened basement corner, I felt the humiliation; shame and despair begin crashing in on me again.
>
> You are better than this . . . You are more than this . . . It was a lovely, deep and wide voice that brought with it the feelings and beautiful knowing of love that I had experienced in my dream.
>
> You know me? I whispered—afraid to ask. Afraid not to ask.
>
> Yes.
>
> I lay in my cot and basked in the healing warmth. I was loved.[8]

---

8   Melissa G. Moore, with M. Bridget Cook, *Shattered Silence: The Untold Story of a Serial Killer's Daughter* (Springville, UT: Cedar Fort Inc., 2009), 52.

Melissa's prayer, "If you know who I am," mirrors my longing to be known. I have watched Nelson's knowing of me slowly fade away. Saying goodbye to his "knowing" requires an evolving adjustment as I search for bits and pieces in other places. That supportive "I'm praying for you" left me listless because it just didn't stack up alongside my longing to be known. Don't just pray for me: know me. Know me, and then pray that I can receive the mystery of God's knowing—that I can hear God's "I know you" as clearly as I once heard Nelson's.

My father loves my mother so much; I can see how this is hurting him to watch her deteriorate. I think at this point, she is no longer grieving at the loss of her motor skills and memory, but we are grieving as we see her slip into a place with which we are not familiar.

—"Linda"

Like you, I need more than prayers. It seems like it's the thing people say out of habit. It seems to make the praying individual feel better.

—"Riley"

How important is it to you to be known? What would you do with that longing in a marriage that included dementia?

Long-term care but still a caregiver

March

The last weeks have blurred together into a collage of images, emotions, and new experiences. On Tuesday, January 26, I was on the walking path with my friend when my cell phone rang. It was a long-term care facility, and they offered a bed for Nelson on Wednesday or Thursday. We had been in touch with them as our second choice.

The next day my sister, Micki, helped me label Nelson's clothes, and on Thursday we moved him in with his new roommate. So many things led up to making this seem like the right time that I felt very peaceful about the decision. When I talked with Nelson about it, he offered no resistance. It was hard to know how much he understood, which added to the sense of timeliness for me.

Now I have to keep reminding myself of all the things that fell into place to make it happen and feel right. I knew intellectually that the transition would be hard, but I didn't know in reality what that meant. I am finding out.

My friend who has walked this road ahead of me told me I wouldn't stop being a caregiver when Nelson was in a nursing home. She was right. With my sister's help, we try to manage his quality of life. That means seeing the gaps in his care and doing what we can to fill them. While I knew that he was not going to get one-on-one care, I wasn't prepared for how many gaps there would be.

Nelson loves ice cream, but he missed the ice cream social. What happened? Another day he was wearing his roommate's clothes. Does it matter? He told me he wasn't sure if this was his toothbrush. What to do about it? We'd asked that someone remind him to rest after lunch, but we don't know if anyone does. Now what? Multiple combs have disappeared and been replaced. What's the solution? He struggles to feed himself. Will anyone step in to help? I walked into his shared bathroom to see him drinking water from a denture cup. He doesn't wear dentures. We brought a familiar cup from home and marked his name on it with nail polish. Will that work? I walked in one day to find him sitting all alone in the lobby and looking very sad. He was feeling the loss of this change but needed help to express it. What if I hadn't come?

We need to keep communicating with staff as we try to assure adequate care. Meanwhile, Nelson and I are both dealing with feelings of loss and trying to adapt emotionally. It's another phase of letting go in this relentless goodbye. I did my best but now the time has come for full-time care and my heart still asks why. I wonder if he will forget all about me if I don't come in often enough. Will his other caregivers replace me? Does he feel abandoned?

On these snowy winter days, the Nelson I once knew would be out with me and some borrowed grandkids building a snowman or making an igloo. I grieve again the loss of my own youthfulness and health during these past years as I have focused on surviving caregiving. I wonder what I have to look forward to while I live in a perpetual state of letting go.

The move to long-term care seems to have created longer lasting swings into lower function. Do we assume that it is all due to disease progression? Or is he pushing himself beyond endurance because he enjoys the people that are always around? We've scheduled in more naps and that has helped.

There's a lot of trial and error. We can keep a close eye on things and go back to what we did all along, our best. We just keep on with the caregiving, attempting to meet his needs, as well as our own, as best we can. That's what caregivers do.

Thank you for your words. They speak volumes about what it means to love, to lose, to cope, to help another even when it feels like it's killing us.
— "Rachel"

With dementia it seems the present day is better than tomorrow.

—"Katie"

What were your feelings after your first visit to someone in a nursing home? Did you go back after the first visit? Why or why not? If you were involved in their care, what was it like? If you have struggled with the quality of nursing home care, how have you responded?

Finding Nelson

_____

April

We're two months into the nursing home experience. Nelson often doesn't know his way around and frequently walks past his room or the door to the dining room. He forgets that there is a bathroom in his room. Now this partner of mine who never forgot a face or a name doesn't know the names of people he sees every day. He's lost much of the time, not knowing where he is or why he's there.

Two weeks ago the staff called me at home to say that Nelson was agitated, uncooperative, and combative. Would I talk to him? Unable to get a handle on what he needed, I told him and the staff I'd come in to see him. When I arrived around 9 p.m., I was met by the head nurse. "This is so not like Nelson," I said. She reassured me, saying they understood that brain changes were manifesting a different Nelson. I agreed.

Now I look back and wonder if this was more the real Nelson than we thought. There had been no medication changes, so we couldn't blame behavior changes on the meds. But he had been put into a totally strange environment without the ability to problem solve and remember. For a month or so, his manners and good nature overrode his fears. But then with the inability to express his fears and needs, perhaps hallucinations, or perhaps an impatient or demanding aide, Nelson's true self was threatened beyond tolerance. He knew only that he was lost and did not like the way he was being treated. The real Nelson knew this is not the way things are supposed to be. His only recourse was to resist.

Now he has been given new meds, one for anxiety and one for sleep. Though he still indicates he doesn't want to be there, he usually responds cooperatively to gentleness and patient interactions that preserve his dignity, which can take huge chunks of staff time. At the same time, he has difficulty verbalizing his needs or trusting strangers enough to tell them the things that are worrying him. It's hard on the pride to admit to a stranger that you're afraid, lost, or confused.

Nelson is so camouflaged these days by LBD's haze that at times I think we've lost him completely. But if I'm alert and patient, now and again I get to enjoy a moment of clarity or a shine of the old Nelson.

This morning, after helping him with breakfast, I put him in a lounge chair in the activity room with the newspaper. I told him I was going to leave and would be back later in the day. He wanted to know what time.

"At four-thirty I'll be back," I said.

"Here?" He questioned anxiously.

"I'll see you in your room," I said because that's usually where he is when I get there in the late afternoon. Then, noting his anxiety, I added, "I'll find you wherever you are." That's when he broke into the biggest grin I've seen in weeks.

Reassurances, I've discovered, are crucial. It may be "Good job" no matter how small the task he has done; or my hand lightly rubbing his back telling him I'm there to help when needed; or a quick "It's ok" when a noise startles him.

No matter what, Nelson, I will find you.

They took such good care of him. He was falling at home, resisted daycare, and was so angry and frustrated. He couldn't eat, dress, or shower by himself, and it was time. I know I not only did the right thing for him, but I did the right thing for me. I'm at peace now and I know he no longer has to struggle.

—"Karen"

Having dementia has been compared to being in a foreign country where you can't understand the language. If you have ever been in that situation, what was it like? How would thinking about dementia in that way change your way of being with someone who has dementia?

How many times can you say goodbye?

May

When a friend whose husband died of complications from LBD wrote to tell me about the beautiful day and the perfect ceremony when they gathered to inter her husband's ashes, I thought again about all the good-byes that we caregivers of spouses with LBD have had to say.

Before I knew Nelson had a disease, we were beginning to struggle in our relationship. Why did we argue so often? Why did we feel so distant? Why couldn't we communicate effectively? Something was wrong, but I couldn't uncover what it was.

When Nelson was struggling with his teaching job, I began to communicate with his principal. She affirmed that there were problems that had to be resolved in order for him to return the following year. I think it was then that I said my first goodbye to the competent man I had married. It was then I began consciously to function for him.

We both resisted that goodbye. He couldn't see why he shouldn't go back to teaching. He also had to say the first of many goodbyes: goodbye to making his own decisions. I had to begin to override his decisions.

It was a killing goodbye. I loved his solidness. I loved his confidence, his comfort with himself and his choices. I had to take over that part of him, and it put a wedge between us. I said goodbye to my dependence on his good judgment.

I knew there would never be a recovery. We could help him compensate for a while, have him write things down, use a datebook, but gradually he was unable to rely on memory and observation. He would forget to look at his datebook, and it would be discarded. He couldn't remember what he did last week, and then yesterday, and then an hour ago. Goodbyes piled up in front and behind.

After his driving became erratic, I had to step in and override his judgment. Goodbye to counting on him to help with the checkbook, house maintenance, car maintenance, and lawn care. Eventually even taking out the garbage was removed from the list. Then I had to stop asking him to bring me something from the next room. Goodbye. The list of things he could do to help diminished to nothing.

Early on, communication became a monumental task. He might say "Bring me a chair," when he meant "Bring me a stool." When I brought the chair, he would be frustrated. It strangled our easy way of living together. Goodbye. We distanced from each other in order to cope. Goodbye. Then we would come back together and try again with similar results.

His ability to mesmerize others with funny stories disappeared. He'd start the story and forget an important detail, but not realize it. He'd laugh while we, his family or friends, would politely laugh along to cover up our puzzlement. Another goodbye unfolding.

Problem solving escaped him, and when he tried to hang on to that ability, craziness happened. The shelves he tried to build ran cattywampus. The mower he tried to fix ended up more damaged after his efforts. He once put gas in the car with the engine running. Goodbye, goodbye, goodbye.

When he couldn't organize his medications, I began to do it. Then he couldn't remember to take the medications, so I gave them to him and watched to make sure he swallowed. After more years, I began to put them in his mouth and hold the cup for him. Another goodbye. Yet another item falls irretrievably onto the pile of losses. Goodbye.

While we caregivers are trying to adjust to each goodbye, the disease keeps teasing us with moments of higher functioning. These on-again, off-again goodbyes take their toll on both partners.

Somewhere along the way we caregivers realize that we have neither the perks of marriage nor the perks of being single. We do, however, have the responsibilities of both. Even more confusing is that we are now like a parent to our spouse. All these confusing new roles require emotional gymnastics in order to cope, and we have to say goodbye to every expectation.

I suspect my friend's goodbye on that beautiful day will not be her last. But I would be surprised if she told me it was the hardest. People tell me I'm strong. Saying the relentless goodbye for years on end either makes you tough or it breaks you. But now I am wondering, how many times can you say goodbye without breaking?

How do you mourn for someone that keeps leaving but comes back for a while? When we lose a spouse, we mourn and know it is permanent, but LBD just puts you through that old rollercoaster ride losing them a hundred times over and over. After a while I find it harder and harder to pick myself up and start again no matter how short the good was.
— Rita McAdam

He is not sleeping. He sees things. He sees things like a dog sleeping on the foot of his bed. Also he grabs for things in the air. His swallowing is getting bad. But part of me wishes that he would just go to sleep rather than see him go like this. My mum is going to have another nervous breakdown.
— "Julia"

What are some of the most difficult goodbyes you have had to say in your life? What made them hard? What got you through that goodbye? How do you think you would handle the long goodbye of dementia?

The hardest thing

June

During my nearly twenty years of caregiving, I have often heard myself say, "The hardest thing is . . ." But each time I'd say it, there would be a different ending. What is the hardest thing? I could never decide.

Recently I thought the hardest thing was discovering that I've grown old. My hair is much whiter. My body lags far behind my intentions, and it protests at tasks that were once effortless. Now I am finding that the things I'm capable of doing are falling away at an alarming speed. It's easy to think that there is little to look forward to.

But there is one thing, I believe, that trumps and perhaps includes all the endings. It is the grieving of losses. And as the years go by, each loss gets bigger and is revisited over and over again.

Harold Ivan Smith says, "The goal of wise grief is not to 'get over' or 'move on.' The goal is to learn from the experience. The goal is to integrate the experience into the fabric of our story. The goal is to live although grieving."[9] The hardest thing is to live for five or ten or fifteen years, all the while grieving. I once met a couple about my age whose only children were their two adult sons—both severely disabled and in wheelchairs. The parents had cared for them since they were born. We had an instant connection, not because I can even imagine what it's like to be in their shoes, but because we both live in a grief that is suspended in time with reminders that never go away.

Most people pass in and out of painful experiences and may even grieve a long time because of them. But at some point, there is usually the potential for putting energy and life into other hopeful experiences. When reminders of your loss are ongoing, you remain in a sustained grief that wears away resilience.

What does living while grieving look like? A grief specialist once explained that grief is how we feel about a loss. Mourning is how we express what we feel. Everyone grieves. Not everyone mourns. To heal we must mourn, she said.

For me, the hardest thing is to live while mourning. It means having time and place for the expression of shock, sadness, anger, frustration, and fear—all elements of grieving. It means journaling, crying, raging, keening, talking to a good listener, praying, and doing whatever it takes to express the grief.

Grief counselors and grief groups speak of shifting emotional energy to new relationships after a loved

---

9. Harold Ivan Smith, "You gotta be going there to get there." (*Journeys*, Hospice Foundation of America newsletter: October 2005), 2.

one dies. But I needed help with the grief of letting go of the relationship we once had and forging the best possible relationship with Nelson, who was still physically alive and present. I needed help to redefine our relationship. Who was I now? Who were we now? What would this mean for me? For us?

In her book *Ambiguous Loss*,[10] Pauline Boss recognizes the difficulty and the ambivalence of grief when someone becomes emotionally unavailable but is still physically present; when grief is fractured and murky. I was heartened to see the attention Boss's book gave to the disconnect between my grief and that of those mourning the finality of death.

For spousal caregivers who are faced daily with their losses, mourning is part of the job. For us, mourning is a critical part of living. We live. We give care. We love. We laugh if we can, and we must mourn. That is the hardest thing—the growing loss, the incessant grief, and the mourning that by necessity is an ongoing part of our experience.

The hardest thing I am dealing with is that he believes I am having sex with all these men he sees right in front of him. The accusing words and hurt he truly feels are almost unbearable for me.

—"Ann"

10. Pauline Boss, *Ambiguous Loss: Learning to Live with Unresolved Grief* (Cambridge: Harvard University Press, 1999).

I mourned daily, every minute, for years while he was still breathing. It's almost as though there are no words to describe the life of a caregiver.

—"Inez"

I know I grieve, but I am not so sure I mourn.

—"Philip"

It was so hard to see the man I married change into a very old, old man who was so not the man he used to be. He died almost ten months ago. It was a very long hard journey. He did not ask for such a terrible end and I did not either. But I stayed the course and so did he. Now I have no regrets for caring for him and I know he blesses my future and wishes the best for me.

—"Raylene"

Think of a time when you had to "live while grieving." What was it like? What did you learn from living in grief?

Maybe this is mercy

July

She tells me her blood pressure is over two hundred even though she is on medication. She walks to the nursing home to visit her husband, Nelson's roommate, even though the temperature outdoors has been in the nineties. She's not sure how far it is but from what she says, I calculate it must be at least two miles. She says her doctor warned her that if she doesn't get her blood pressure down she will die before he does. He is ninety. We stand there between our sleeping husbands, our eyes locked in knowing, pain-filled silence. Mine fill with tears.

"You are so young," she says. The tears spill over.

I'm young and I'm the one that wants to sit down. I pull out Nelson's lounge chair and the screech interrupts the silence. We both wince. I tell her to sit down but she doesn't want to make any noise to pull in another chair. She doesn't mind standing, she says. She leans in close each time I talk so that she can hear. I remember the folding chair we keep stowed behind the curtain and pull it out. She sits on that.

She talks then about his back injury, marriage to him, how they have blended their lives. Then we discover that we have something else in common. She is also chemically sensitive. She is fragrance free except for her shampoo. I tell her it's hard to find but I get it at Raisin Rack. "It's expensive," I say.

Without hesitation she gets up, brings out her purse and hands me a ten. The store is in the opposite direction of her neighborhood. I'm glad to buy it for her.

But I do it for me as well. It's been an especially difficult summer. Being outdoors usually provides respite from my chemical sensitivities. Summer has always been my healthy season. I work in my flower beds, bring friends to my porch swing, sit by the woods to watch the birds, go for frequent accompanied walks, and attend outdoor reunions with less worry about allergic reactions to fragrances. The loneliness of the long, closed-in winter is for a time forgotten. This year, however, we have had more than the usual rain, heat, and humidity. Everyone says allergies are worse. My breathing gets labored after being outside. Now I'm indoors with windows closed and shades drawn to keep out the stifling hot sun. My sense of loneliness at home has grown. I pray for mercy. "Where are you, God?"

My faith wanes. Unanswered questions about God and suffering seem suspended, hanging on a precarious bit of hope. I'm waiting. Waiting to know who this God is who seems so comfortable with suffering. Wanting some reassurance that life is not just a series of unhappy accidents. Hoping daily for some small thing that day to strengthen hope.

Maybe this nearly fragrance-free Romanian wife is mercy. We moved Nelson to this room because his old room was getting a new floor. Odors from the floor would have made it unsafe for me. Mid-move we discovered fragrance dispensers in the new room. I'm highly allergic to their fragrance. We threw them out. Housekeeping washed down the walls twice with vinegar water and changed the curtains. I brought in an air cleaner and hoped the heating and cooling unit in the room wasn't throwing fragrance into the air.

"We need help," she says. "I don't think any person can help us." Her eyes are dry but overflow with sadness. "I'm ready for heaven," she adds.

Maybe she who mirrors my own life—fighting for her health, for her husband's welfare and trying her best to stave off loneliness—is the mercy I asked for. Maybe she, who understands my struggle with aging, illness, and loss, is here to share a little solace in the waiting for greater faith and hope. Maybe together we will find hope strengthened. Maybe this is mercy.

I spent the first six months after my husband died in a state of euphoria, thinking that if this was widowhood, it was a cakewalk. Then the crash of his loss hit. When I finally realized that I needed more help adjusting, I sought out a grief counselor. One of the first things she suggested was talking to him out loud and not just in my head. It felt odd

at first, but I realized that I already unconsciously talked to him aloud whenever something funny happened.

—Renata Rafferty

In what circumstance has your faith waned or been tested? What is mercy to you? In what current situations might you say, "Maybe this is mercy"?

How are you doing?

September

We had a "plan of care" meeting today at the care facility, which is Nelson's home all of the time and mine from 4:30-6:30 each evening. We were told how Nelson walked out of the facility with a visitor. The visitor was not his. A nurse dashed out the door and followed him, but he wasn't interested in going back inside. She walked with him until, as she said, "We went by the same window so many times someone came out to help me."

I told them how he had recently met and remembered with no hesitation the name of a former student —someone he hadn't seen for at least fifteen years. I told them how at my Tuesday evening visit his eyes were open, but he didn't show any signs of recognition. The staff had seen this phenomenon too. He had been sleeping more, eating less, and his eyes were glazed and unresponsive. He had been unable to feed himself.

I told them that the next evening had started out the same. I sat there wondering if this was going to be the new normal and thinking how glad I was that our son and daughter had both been to see him recently when he was still responsive. Then about fifteen minutes before I left, it was as if a switch had been turned on. He opened his eyes, there was recognition, and he spoke to me.

As we sat around the table at the meeting, we shared our wonder at this strange disease and its manifestations. When all seemed to have been said and our concerns had been addressed, there was silence. The social worker looked at me and asked how I was doing. I drew a blank. I couldn't shift my thinking. I didn't know what to say.

How do you begin to talk about the experience of letting go of a spouse one day at a time for years on end? Where are the words to describe the sense of having a husband, but not having a marriage? What do you say about the depression that inevitably colors days or weeks at a time? What do you leave out because you want to protect them from your pain? What do you leave out because you don't want to feel the pain? When, if not now, do you expose the fear of what is going to happen to you? How much do they really want to know? Do they just want reassurance that you are going to keep the faith? Do they see in your face the tiredness you feel from living with loss, the drain you feel from being bounced between hope and despair, the numbness you choose when you can't feel anymore?

So I said something inane. "I vacillate." Then looking for substance, I added, "The house feels so empty." The social worker asked if I see myself moving. "It's inevitable," I responded.

Most revealing to me was how blindsided I was by the question. More often I am asked about Nelson. Nelson and the disease become the focus.

So, how am I doing? Once again I'm recognizing that I have the capacity to do things that I never would have chosen or thought myself capable of doing. I go to bed and get up in a house that screams empty. I do what has to be done: chores and house maintenance, bill paying and shopping; and then at 4:30, I walk into the nursing home wondering what I will find today. I deal with calm or calamity depending on the day. Last night he greeted me with, "I want to be out of here by tonight"—the equivalent of an order articulated with none of his usual groping for words. I have learned to set my emotions on a shelf. I listen, reorient him to his reality, wade with him through his loss, and then come home to an empty house to wade through my own.

How am I doing? Maybe the same responses will have to do. I am better on some days than others. I'm doing as well as can be expected. I'm learning to live in a divided place where faith and doubt constantly collide, where hope and despair live side by side, where joy and sadness are expressed back to back, where love and fear walk hand in hand. That's how I'm doing. And thank you for asking.

I feel like I'm losing him in slow motion. A neighbor lost her husband suddenly, and I felt a certain envy and guilt for thinking how easy that must be. I like positive people, but it is an uphill battle to stay positive.

—"Beth"

Do you ever wonder (as I do), who's going to take care of me? There is the physical side to that and the emotional side. You just want someone to take your hand and tell you everything's going to be all right. But the person who used to do that isn't there.

—Florrie Munat

Do you identify with any of the questions the author asks herself when asked how she is doing? Which ones? Under what circumstances in your life have you found it difficult to respond to inquiries about how you are doing?

Taking care of me

November

We had two extraordinary evenings together. Nelson was alert, relaxed, and smiling. At the end of the second evening when I walked past his window on the way to the car, we blew kisses and shared smiles. It was a level of alertness I hadn't seen in weeks. So it was a jolt back to LBD reality when I arrived the next afternoon to find him sitting on the floor, his back against the bed, asleep. There were multiple chili smudges on his pants. Did any make it to his mouth, I wondered. He looked like a street person hunched over on the floor, his clothes soiled and disheveled. No amount of prodding or saying his name would wake him. When I asked a favorite and usually cheerful nurse if Nelson had had a rough day, she looked up from her paperwork and forcing a half smile said, "Kinda, sorta." It looked like she too had had a rough day. I asked her if he took a nap, and she said they put him down but he kept getting back up.

When I realized he wasn't going to wake for me, the nurse corralled three aides and, with one on each limb, they lifted him onto the bed. Soon after that another younger, more energetic nurse asked me, "How are you doing?" I couldn't hide how I was feeling, and she gave me a little pep talk about taking care of myself.

I've heard this talk often and have given it to other caregivers as well. I know it's true. I know the grim statistics for caregivers. According to the *Journal of the American Medical Association*, "Elderly spousal caregivers (aged 66–96) who experience caregiving-related stress have a 63% higher mortality rate than noncaregivers of the same age."[11] I know it's not selfish to take care of me. I've lived the past ten years taking care of myself. I take it all seriously.

But it is all beginning to amuse me. Maybe it's because I wonder, how else could I have possibly survived this long except by taking care of myself? Or maybe it's because I think, you have no idea how difficult and ridiculous taking care of me gets with my chemical sensitivities on top of the caregiving! Their suggestions often include shopping or manicures; I can do neither because of my chemical sensitivities.

One of the residents calls me the "Bag Lady" because I come into the nursing home carrying multiple bags, which hold things for me to do if Nelson sleeps. There is my mostly organic dinner and my reverse osmosis

---

11. Richard Schulz and Scott R. Beach, "Caregiving as a Risk Factor for Mortality: The Caregiver Health Effects Study." *JAMA: The Journal of the American Medical Association* (1999): 282: 2215–2219.

water. It seems that besides going to the nursing home and performing the keeping-life-together tasks and doing paperwork, all I do is take care of me.

My list of "taking care of me" requirements has grown longer as I've aged. It's no longer just the basics like brushing teeth and washing hands. Now I do at least fifteen minutes of stretching and yoga in the morning. I eat oatmeal. I walk several times a week. For socialization I often persuade someone to walk with me. I wear weights on my ankles several times a week during the winter months to slow down osteopenia rather than take drugs. I take calcium and vitamins.

I eat more organic food, more veggies, less meat, less salt, and more salmon. I have cut out sugar, get plenty of sleep, call friends when I need to talk, do deep breathing to keep my blood pressure down, and meditate to repair cells. PBS says studies show meditation repairs telomeres and slows down aging after all. Since I'm alone a lot, I talk to myself, and answer if I want to. Sometimes I watch *America's Funniest Home Videos* to get a few good laughs. I pray; I try to think positively; and when I feel a loss I mourn it so the grieving doesn't go inside and weigh me down. I look back infrequently and think ahead only if necessary. I mean, how much more taking care of myself can I do?

A friend emailed me, "Take care of yourself. This could be a long haul." I laughed. Could be? Has been! I wrote back and told her I think the way I have survived all these years is by not looking ahead—and added that maybe I'm burying my head in the sand.

She countered with, "As long as the rest of your body doesn't follow!" Good distinction!

Once in a rare while life gives our bodies the gift of health and vitality in spite of our neglect. Caregivers do well to learn quickly that most of us must live life like our lives depend on it.

We well spouses continue to age and the time will come when we are not able to do the active things we wish our spouses could do with us now.

—"Alice"

I realize now that I was grieving all that time not only because of the hardship of being a caregiver, but also for myself and the fact that there wasn't much time left to live the rest of my life without the stress and caregiving.

—"Cheryl"

After my husband's stroke, a friend of my daughter, who works with stroke "survivors" (as they say), told my daughter, "Don't worry about your father; his needs will be met. You should be worrying about your mother whose needs may not be."

—Florrie Munat

How do you do at taking care of yourself? What would you like to do that could improve your self care? Will you do it?

Voices

December

"Talk to me," I heard her plead as I walked into the lobby. "Don't just walk away. You can at least talk to me." She sat in a wheelchair in Nursing Home USA—rated five stars by Medicare—and was speaking to the backside of an aide that was by now far down the hall. The resident's back was to the door I had just entered.

I walked past her, never acknowledging her presence.

What have I become? Am I one of them—the nurses and aides—spread too thin, immersed in helplessness and need, maybe callous or numb?

It's been ten months now since I started making daily nursing home visits to my husband of now forty-four years. Lewy body began showing up twenty years ago in some other life that I now can only faintly remember. Now my hair is white, my body more stiff, and my step more cautious. The possibility of dying before Nelson seems more believable as time marches on.

I'm focused but drained from this life of in-between—caring for him and taking care of me, losing him and holding on to me, full nursing home and empty house, married but alone.

Between visits I want to forget what happens behind those doors: the drink a thirsty resident can't reach, the fear dementia can't express, the hand that reaches out and no one holds, or the tears when a resident tries unsuccessfully to open dinnertime packaging. I don't want to think about the shut-down, bored eyes; or those with no visitors; or the hunger for eye contact, touch, stimulation, and response.

I want to forget the voice of my husband, "I don't know where I am." I want to walk out and not think about all the losses I see for those who have grown old in a culture where youth is god and the aged are sidelined.

I want to walk in and out, focusing on taking care of us—him and me—and on beating the odds for caregiver survival.

But I'm tossed between my need and the needs of all those nursing home residents. They are powerless to make themselves heard. Who will be their voice?

I'm watching myself grow old from some detached place during this twenty-year goodbye. Now he's here, now he's not. Now he's responsive, now he's not. Over and over again. I see myself wearing down, losing resilience. I'm dry-eyed when another wife in tears says she can't go on. Numb and empty. I come empty. I leave empty.

Tonight I've said goodbye to my husband. But a loud, guttural, demanding call of another resident follows me as I start out the door toward home. I turn back to see him, wheelchair bound, imploring me with his eyes. He wants to say goodbye. Words ring in my ears. "At least talk to me."

I go back, squeeze his hand, messy from dinner and who knows what else. "Goodbye, George. I'll see you tomorrow." His eyes shine brighter, his smile grows big. I turn and go home to sit with my sadness.

Who will listen? Who will be their voice?

Is this is the best we can do?

His family has not talked to me because I put him
in the nursing home. But I refuse to go into this
newfound freedom with hatred and bitterness. I can
only do that with Christ's example and help.
—Katherine Holder

How good of a listener are you? Would you consider giving time to visiting and listening to the residents in a nursing home? Why or why not?

YEAR 15

What you gain you lose,
so you might as well enjoy what you have.
—Nelson Burkholder, 2011

"Goodbye," he said, "Stop in again," as if I were some casual
visitor here on a whim.
For forty-three years, I have called him "honey."
Now I visit him in a nursing home,
spoon ice cream into his mouth,
and take what recognition or connection I can get,
as a gift against tomorrow's even further decline,
against some future
"goodbye."
Marriage was the vehicle we entered to move forward and grow
together. When one begins to go in reverse, then what?
No matter how much you want life to stand still it won't. He is
now in reverse and an excruciatingly slow and painful one.
You better know how to mourn.
You better know how to integrate pain and grief and sadness into
your own forward motion life of learning and growing.

—GHB

Happy you, sad me

January

"Psychic yardage" is what Mary Karr in her memoir *The Liars' Club* calls the emotional distance between her sister and herself when they respond with opposite emotions to the same event.[12] This phrase struck a familiar chord with me. During the first five to ten years of Nelson's disease, I was in so much emotional pain I couldn't laugh or even comprehend other people's laughter. The bottom had fallen out of my safe, secure world, and I was in free fall. The jokes were stupid, the games were silly, and much of what everyone else was doing seemed pointless. Laughter always created what seemed like a psychic chasm between me and others.

Thankfully, I survived that free fall and have come through it stronger and much more aware of the color my own perceptions put on life. I'm learning to accept

---

12. Mary Karr, *The Liar's Club: A Memoir*. (New York: Penguin, 1996), 100.

sadness along with happiness, fear along with love, and pain along with contentment as part of life. Long-term spousal caregiving gives abundant opportunity to learn from grief and its entourage of emotions and to learn how to deal with psychic yardage.

As I have observed each new Lewy body dementia (LBD) loss of function, each new loss of potential for connection between Nelson and me, each new loss of support from him, and each new loss of normalcy, I have tallied up lessons about grief and psychic yard-age. I've learned that people can't really understand what they haven't experienced. It's not fair for me to expect them to. I've learned that given the opportunity, people will often empathize, but that requires my will-ingness to be vulnerable.

I find myself feeling the emotional distance in social situations when conversations turn to normal but laughable spousal interactions. She talks about his silly habit, he tells a tale on her—intimacies that are no longer available to me. My feelings quickly turn to sadness and psychic yardage. Laughing you, sad me.

I once listened to a speaker talk about adult relation-ships to an adult audience. He addressed both those who were single and those who were married. I sat there and wondered where I fit in. Not with the cou-ples. Not with the singles. Most of what he said simply did not apply to my relationship with Nelson. When I went up to the speaker afterward and wondered where I fit in this world, he was understandably puzzled.

I briefly told him my story: I've been living with a spouse who has had dementia for over a decade.

He immediately became sympathetic and understood what I wanted him to—that spousal caregivers have a unique and rarely addressed dilemma. We don't fit. We aren't seen. We live with psychic yardage.

I've learned that there are things I can do to minimize the psychic yardage. Sometimes when I find myself skidding into grief-producing psychic yardage, I remove myself. I don't need to stay in a room full of couples talking about their travels to distant parts of the world, or their grand wedding anniversaries.

Other times, sharing my private grief with another person builds understanding. I've cultivated relationships with people who understand and welcome the healing power of grieving and mourning so that vulnerability on both sides is part of the relationship. This, more than anything else, has kept me from the misery of alienation that threatens with chronic psychic yardage.

As spousal caregivers, we have to find ways to promote understanding when we can't participate in the party. We have to live our grief authentically so that we will come through the pain stronger and be able to join an occasional party without being a drag on it.

The truth about life for all of us is that it holds both joy and sadness. Holding on to them both loosely keeps me sane in the precarious world of spousal caregiving and sometimes allows for a precious moment when I blend with the "normal" world and there is no psychic yardage at all.

Wow! And I thought it was just me—why I always feel like a fifth wheel.

—"Amanda"

I spent the first two months of the year caring for him in his home. The man I knew was all but gone. I have now decided to rejoice when he has a great day and deal with those days that are not. If you have no experience with it, you cannot begin to understand how difficult daily life as a caregiver is.

—Cyndi Foley

In what situations have you experienced "psychic yardage"?

Promises, promises

March

Nelson and I were married on a fall evening in a small-ish country church where yew shrubs greeted the guests as the sun loped to the west. "Together God and I will take real good care of you," Nelson had written to me three months earlier.

At our wedding, friends sang a song based on words from the biblical story of Ruth:

> Where you go, I will go;
> Where you lodge, I will lodge;
> Your people shall be my people
> And your God my god.
>
> —Ruth 1:15

Today, I mutter things under my breath when I hear young lovers pledge unconditional love, or pronounce expectations that they will always be together with their love. You don't know, I say to myself. You wait and see. It's just not that simple or easy.

When Nelson became agitated and combative soon after we placed him in the nursing home, the nurse had said she understood it was the disease and that they were here to walk with me "all the way to the end." I was touched by that commitment, but eleven months later I began to get the uncomfortable feeling that they might ask him to go elsewhere. Unlike most residents, Nelson on good days is quick on his feet. He had walked out about once a week for several weeks, either following a visitor out the door or walking out of doors that had no alarms. The nurse's promise seemed to be in jeopardy.

My sister, Micki, and I did everything we could to make it work. Micki, Nelson's friend Murray, and I regularly put in between three to five hours of visits and care each weekday. We also worked with the ombudsperson who is trained to help ensure a resident's care and serves as a go-between with families and the nursing home. Our ombudsperson was an invaluable resource. She enlisted the nursing home staff in strategies to address his restlessness. It wasn't enough and as exits became more frequent, my worst fears became reality.

The nursing home recommended admitting Nelson to a small geriatric psych ward where medications might be fine-tuned. From there he could be admitted to a skilled care facility of our choosing where there was a secure dementia care unit. A patient in a facility's skilled care takes precedence for admission to an available dementia care bed over someone from the outside. As it turned out he could have gone straight to the facility and saved a whole lot of grief for everyone.

Because we know the danger of anti-psychotics with LBD, and their possibly irreversible effects, Micki and I had emphasized to psych staff that we did not want new medications introduced without our consent. We were assured in an offhand sort of way that we would be notified. Still, the doctor started him on an antipsychotic. When we registered our dismay, the doctor cut the dosage in half and then discontinued it.

After ten days in the psych ward, it was time to travel the sixty miles to Nelson's new home. We did not trust the seatbelt as an adequate restraint as he rode in the front passenger seat. I had a wide winter scarf, and from my place in the back seat I wrapped it around him and tied him into the seat. Once he was in the new facility, we discovered scabs all down the front of his shins, which added to my belief that the psych ward is not a place for those with dementia.

During his first two weeks in this new facility, he had episodes of agitation and combativeness. The staff gave him Depakote, a mood stabilizer, and Melatonin to help him sleep. After he managed to walk out a few times, the facility beefed up the security system, which seemed to help.

We started out with a promise to stay together and to care for each other but now our lives are worlds apart. Now we are together only in the broadest sense of the word. He wonders where he is. I search for meaning in why he is there. Dreams and hallucinations confuse him, an intrusion I can't imagine. I don't know what it's like to be unable to distinguish dream from reality or unable to tell someone that you are thirsty. I don't know if he is as tortured in that shaking, unco-operative body as I believe I would be. I just can't go there. I can't walk in those shoes and he can't walk in mine. This new facility is twenty miles from home, so now we add physical miles to our separation. Life has given us circumstances that push us into compromise.

I once read about a caregiver who told his spouse that her job was to enjoy life and his was to manage it. This implied to me that there is no enjoyment for the caregiver. I now give Nelson a revised message: "We're retired. Our job is to enjoy ourselves as much as we can." Maybe I tell him this because Nelson might have a hard time let-ting me be the "manager." Or maybe it acknowledges my own need to find enjoyment beyond the managing. "Everything is taken care of," I often reassure him. But I sometimes think: If he only knew. But he can't know. It all fosters a brittle togetherness and strains the promises.

Now we connect on the basis of our history together and what we've shared. The love it fostered is our bond. Somehow with that bond we hold on to each other. But it is a tenuous hold. A promise will not be enough to keep his memory alive and eventually our history together will elude him.

When all nuances of reciprocal love have disap-peared, and when history and promises are gone from memory, then what? I don't know. But I know prom-ises keep me going. Not so much the promise I made forty-four years ago, but the occasional responsive touch or smile from the one who through our shared history has become as familiar and comfortable as an old pair of shoes. A few weeks ago in a walk down the nursing home hall, he put his arm around my waist. The moment was one of sweet comfort. I can't discard the hope of that comfort and connection. I can't discard those old shoes. I just can't, promise or no promise.

I treasure a photo that I keep on my desk—the one with a mischievous twinkle in his eye—the real person, with a ready wit and zest for life—he who sent forty daisies to my office on our fortieth anniversary when the popular song was, "I'll Give You a Daisy a Day, Dear." Promises, promises.

—Verna Farr

Yesterday morning I went to my husband's room and said my usual "rise and shine." He didn't reply; he had passed away—but first he had let the cat go out. What a shock! I can't believe it.

—"Carla"

What circumstances have led you to compromise on promises that you had once made? How did you feel about that?

Give feelings a voice

May

We met for lunch in a darkened Macaroni Grill with music that was too loud for my sensitive ears. There were four of us wives, caregivers to husbands with dementia. I remember little about our time together except that I had a soft spot in my heart for Angie, who had been a teacher like Nelson, and who had especially connected with him. Only a few months later, I received a phone call informing me that Angie had unexpectedly passed away. My first thought was of that lunch, for it was the last time I had seen her.

Recently a caregiver asked me, "How do you handle the fear that your husband's illness will actually kill you?" The fear is legitimate according to JAMA, which says that caregivers have a higher mortality rate than their non-caregiving peers.[13]

---

13. Richard Schulz and Scott R. Beach, "Caregiving as a Risk Factor for Mortality: The Caregiver Health Effects Study." *JAMA: The Journal of the American Medical Association* (1999): 282: 2215–2219.

By the time we caregivers hear a diagnosis that predicts years of decline in our spouse, we usually have already been struggling for some time with the confusing new-dementia-driven behaviors. Initially, focusing on changing roles and growing incapabilities, while accommodating the behavioral changes keeps us occupied and it's impossible to even begin to think about our own physical or emotional well-being. What is happening to our health, our fears, and grief just doesn't make it to the top of the list.

But I think how we handle our fears and grief may be a huge determining factor in our survival.

I'm nearly twenty years into living with a spouse altered by LBD. During the first ten years, my fears were big, many, unnamed, and paralyzing. I was the kind of person who wanted to be in the background blending in and letting my very capable husband be the projection of who we were as a couple. I did things independent of him, if needed; I dug my heels into some social peace and justice causes that he didn't have time for, but I liked chasing life with him beside me.

When he was diagnosed, the world suddenly felt lonely and hostile. I couldn't have verbalized it then, but I became at fifty-two a very lost little girl. I truly believed that I could not survive. I would have recurring dreams of being lost on the road or in a big city and unable to find my way home.

Of all the events in my life, the one in which I have unwaveringly seen God's hand was a Sunday school teacher who seemingly came out of nowhere and began to help me name and face my fears. They were

242

many. "Give them a voice," she said to me over and over again. At first, even my tears were silent with gulps and swallows to keep them down. But with her encouragement I began to "give it a voice." I began to peek into a dark black hole of fear and grief and give words to what was there. "There is no one to help me. I am not important. I will always be alone. No one can love me. I can't do this. I'm not enough. No one cares. I have to do it alone. I can't ask for help. I will always be inadequate. I will never figure it out." And on and on. Naming and acknowledging these beliefs was the first step to awareness and giving them a voice.

To express my fears and grief I began journaling. I spoke without edit to the page, not to share with anyone but to increase my own self-awareness and give voice to the fears and the grief. I wrote every day—three pages or more for months. Sometimes it became a prayer journal. Sometimes it became a letter to my inner self, that frightened little girl that had come back to haunt me.

I met with an additional support group facilitated by that life-saving Sunday school teacher. As we did in the Sunday-school-class-like-no-other, this group also learned to speak and listen to each other's fears, at the same time looking for the false beliefs, and nurturing each other to support healthier ways of thinking. Speaking the fears in a confidential setting with others brought those fears down in size and instead of driving others away, as we all feared, it created an incredible bond. We became each other's lifelines.

As I spoke my fears aloud, my voice for speaking truth became stronger. "You don't have to do it alone.

You do matter. You will be okay. You will figure it out. You have more strength than you know. You have options you haven't thought of. You will find a way. You are loved." Over the first years of LBD diagnosis, as I met with these groups, I began to grow and heal. I began to see myself and my brave support group friends, who were all there for reasons other than dementia, become healthier more capable people in a variety of challenges.

Expressing grief for the losses that accompanied my fears was another step to giving voice to my fears. I was and am losing my husband in an excruciating seesaw between here again, gone again, capable now, now not capable, alert one minute, lost the next. I've had to consistently give voice to the feelings triggered by loss in order to keep moving forward.

"Emotional tears," says Judith Orloff, MD, "contain stress hormones which get excreted from the body through crying. . . . emotional tears shed these hormones and other toxins which accumulate during stress. Additional studies also suggest that crying stimulates the production of endorphins, our body's natural pain killer and 'feel-good' hormones." She also says, "The new enlightened paradigm of what constitutes a powerful man and woman is someone who has the strength and self-awareness to cry."[14]

And so I give it a voice. In the first years there would be times when I feared I would never stop crying. As

---

14. Judith Orloff MD, "The Health Benefits of Tears." *The Huffington Post* internet newspaper (July 21, 2010): www.huffingtonpost.com/Judith-orloff-md/emotional wellness_b_653754.html.

I heal and grow stronger, I find the tears come easily, but they also go away more quickly. I name and face the fears more quickly. I feel the loss, and I more easily express my grief and move on. And I can laugh. I know now how much I can survive. I know now that I have a voice that has the power to speak for me and take care of me. I want to beat the odds and so I give the fear and grief a voice. I do it for me and I pray that all caregivers find their voices for grief and truth and making it through and surviving stronger than ever.

Each day is a challenge; we are making it and taking it one day at a time. I pray for strength and wisdom each day, and just do my best. I certainly miss our lives/my life, though. What a horrendous disease this is!

—"LeeAnn"

I struggle daily with new loss as my husband slips away.

—"Regina"

What do you do with loss? Do you minimize it, explain it away, deflect it with humor, or do you give it expression? If you avoid expressing grief, what fear keeps you from doing so? If you express grief, what works best for you?

A cleaner grief

July

I took a four-day reprieve from seeing Nelson. I did nothing out of the ordinary—just the things that get shoved to the bottom of the list on ordinary days.

I carry a small notebook in which I write for each day what I need to remember, where I need to go, what I need to pick up, take along, deposit, the time of appointments, and the times I take my antihistamines if needed. Everything I need to remember is in my notebook.

At the end of the day on Saturday in this four-day stretch, I looked at my notebook and there was nothing on it, but I had been in motion all day. So I wrote in big scrawly letters, "Clean everything. Don't go anywhere." It's what I'd done and it felt good.

By contrast, the years before diagnosis, there was so much messiness. In the summer of 1995, Nelson had finished his twenty-first year of teaching elementary school. Floundering for some direction, I called the principal to see what she had observed. Nelson was always well liked, but the principal believed that something was wrong. "He goes through the lunch line every day and to the teacher's lounge, and then every day he has to go back and get his fork," she told me. "Don't let him come back until he gets help." I asked if she would meet with us so that she could be the one to tell him this. She agreed and tactfully but clearly told him he needed to find out what was going on and get help before he came back.

A few weeks later we sat under our maple tree husking an abundant supply of sweet corn from our garden when he casually said, "I think I'll go back to teaching in the fall."

What should I do? Is God hearing me? Who is this confusing person I'm living with? I was caught in a spin cycle of fear, disbelief, and anger at my circumstances and at the position I was put into in our marriage relationship. I had to repeatedly tell him he couldn't go back and this scenario played out at intervals over the years.

In 1997, with the finality of diagnosis, the waves of grief became brutal and overwhelming. More questions erupted. I had gradually begun to take on a responsibility I did not want for everything that did or did not happen in his life and mine. These waves took me out for days and weeks at a time. I functioned but I was crumbling inside. My toolbox for dealing with what was happening was not well equipped. I hid the fears, swallowed the sadness, displaced the anger, and was stuck in disbelief and shock.

The grief was complex, complicated by a tangle of confusing emotions and questions. How can this be happening? How can I accept this? Who am I, parent or spouse? What happened to "do right and everything will be all right"? This isn't right by any definition I have. I need him. I need him to be capable. He wanted more than anything else to believe he was capable. I didn't want the job of taking away what he resisted giving up, like driving, his teaching job, even communication.

We took a mower part to the store, and as we stood at the counter the male attendant kept looking at Nelson and talking to him. I had removed the part. I had the part in my hands. I knew what was needed. Nelson didn't, but he needed to think he did. He inaccurately explained our problem to the Parts Guy. I wrestled the conversation away from Nelson and eventually made my point without actually saying to the Parts Guy, "You have to talk to me." It hurt me for Nelson. It made me angry for me. It wasn't fair.

Acceptance evolved slowly with help from counselors, friends, support groups, and mentors. Being "good" doesn't mean "bad" things will never happen. People with illness or disability are of no less value. I'm capable of a lot more than I think. I don't have to do it alone.

Acceptance grew as I added new and improved tools of coping. I've learned to ask for help. I've learned to speak my needs. I've learned to be more truthful to myself and others. I've learned to pay attention to what I tell myself about things. Most days, I've stopped telling myself that I don't have choices and can now tell myself I have choices I haven't even thought of yet.

Today the grief is cleaner, not as encumbered by the beliefs that are roots to resistance. Now as waves of sadness wash over me, I more easily acknowledge and express them and they pass more quickly. Grief colors my life but doesn't overwhelm or confuse me as often.

Acceptance doesn't mean I never feel sad. It just means I don't resist the sadness as much when it comes. Acceptance is hard won. It has to be worked at and nurtured. It is sadness for a loss without the encumbering denial, anger, fear, bargains, and resentment.

Acceptance is like a bath. It feels clean and invigorating, but as sure as you are living, you will run into some dirty stuff again; you will fall back into an old pattern of coping or fall back into an old belief.

Then we need to go through the washer of life again, through the agitating pain, and through the soggy grief. If we can let life clean us up, change old ways of thinking, adjust expectations, and not go anywhere every so often, not run from the process, then we can experience a cleaner grief—we can experience greater acceptance.

The dilemma so many of us face is we feel grief at a spouse's "death." The person is gone; we need to mourn. But we're blocked. For the body—which both is and looks like the body that once housed our lost loved one—is right there.

—John C. Jacobs

How difficult is it for you to share your emotions?
Do you have someone with whom you are able to
be vulnerable? If so, in what ways does this person
respond?

No words for his grief

October

Outside my window the October sun shines brightly on a scantily clad maple tree that has shown off its fall color for each of the twenty-five years I have lived here. Change is in the air. The few bright and colorful leaves that stubbornly cling to the branches show hues that I know will soon be gone. These holdouts will fall as all the others have and will become part of an eternal cycle. The cycle reminds us that life has its way, and death and change are a part of living.

For many years Nelson's mother was our last living parent. While he was still living at home, he started asking to call her each week. From the nursing home, these calls were not as easy to make but continued to be important to him. When her death was imminent, I began preparing him for what was to come. I was afraid when the time came he would want to go to the out-of-state funeral. I was unsure if this would be in his best interest. She was buried a week ago at the age of ninety-eight. When I told him about her death, we talked briefly and he said little. I didn't detect any emotion, so I steered him toward the patio. He asked for a tissue and blew his nose, but I attributed it to a cold I suspected he may be getting.

The day of the funeral was a perfect warm and balmy fall day. Without mentioning the funeral, I took Nelson from the nursing home for a snail's pace drive through the nearby Beech Nature Preserve. His thirsty gaze seemed to drink in the fall colors. I knew his alertness took energy and I was prepared for him to lose focus and fall asleep early on, but it didn't happen. He stayed alert as we drove back to the nursing home. Then I was sure he would fall asleep through lunch, but he didn't. We called our daughter. He stayed awake. We called our son. He stayed awake and even chuckled. Then he was ready for a nap.

After a few more days, Nelson asked me how Betty was doing. Nelson's brother Delbert and his wife, Betty, had moved Nelson's mother into their home and had been taking care of her for several years before her death. I told him we would find out. But I started to wonder how Nelson was doing. Was that the real source of the question?

A few fall days went by as I attended to a broken lawn mower, a computer issue, and a stray kitten who was trying desperately to adopt me. But my inner voice told me that I needed to talk to Nelson about how he was doing.

I watched for the opportunity. It came as I read an email to him from Betty saying she was doing okay, but there was a big hole left behind with his mother's absence. I finished reading and looked at Nelson sitting next to me in his chair. He turned toward the baby doll that I held in my lap and, his face pouring love into hers, said, "You know, I love you very much. You know that, don't you?" I watched and tried to know what he was feeling. I asked him then how he was doing with his mother's death.

He began to cry, and for the next few minutes we held each other and cried, the baby doll between us, and then I began to talk. "Life is hard sometimes. We didn't plan that it would be this way. But I want you to know I love you very much." I kept talking about pain, sadness, life, expectations, faith, and his reality. I reminded him that the mess in the bathroom that morning wasn't his fault. I wondered if anything I was saying was what he needed to hear and so I asked, "Is this helping or making it worse?"

"Oh yes," he said, his inflection appreciative but the words indistinguishable.

"It helps?"

He nodded.

It slowly dawned on me that his feelings of loss and grief needed expression. With his inability to verbalize, he had little option to give voice to his losses and therefore could experience little motion toward acceptance and peace. He was going to need me to do the verbalization.

After naming his losses, followed by bursts of sadness and tears, I began to recite Psalm 23 and he joined in. I began to sing "Children of the Heavenly Father." He joined in, and we sang several old familiar songs together. We were having our own little memorial service.

I had brought a notebook of the songs we had been singing together the last few weeks. I pulled it out of my bag and showed it to him. The mood turned lighter as we sang each one, including "Bill Grogan's Goat." It's a great song for him because he can sing the echo.

I read him the words to a song I had recently heard. I had identified with it in many ways and thought it might validate some of his feelings as well. It was Brandi Carlile's "The Story":

All of these lines across my face
Tell you the story of who I am,
So many stories of where I've been,
And how I got to where I am,
But these stories don't mean anything,
When you've got no one to tell them to. . . .[15]

I thought of his inability to tell his stories, happy or sad, and how in spite of his great effort others often can't understand him. I thought of the lines that have formed on my face during the past twenty years. I thought of the empty house where no one waits to hear my story at the end of the day.

We did some nursery school songs with the doll babies and then he stood up and headed toward the door of his room. His interest had moved to something else. He was done grieving and mourning for now. I

15. Lyrics and YouTube video available at: www.lyricsmania.com/the_story_lyrics_brandi_carlile.html (accessed February 22, 2012).

was no longer needed. I could tell by his demeanor, his expression, and his response to my question, "Is it okay if I leave now?" I was relieved.

After my visit with Nelson, halfway to the car, I found myself barely able to move forward as I leaned into a strong cold wind that promised more change. It feels like I do a lot of leaning into the wind these days. But change comes with life, life comes with change, and when we accept that, we are pretty much ready for leaning into anything.

This illness has filled him with anger that keeps boiling to the surface. In Psalm 23 the phrase "He restoreth my soul" has become a lifeline, a promise I hold to for both of us.

—"Beth"

How do you respond when someone else gives grief a voice? Why do you think you respond the way you do? Is your way of responding to grief supportive, or does it minimize or dismiss pain?

Going forward

November

I arrive at the nursing home tired because of a restless night. The aides tell me they have just put Nelson to bed and that he had been restless and worrying about me. His eyes flutter open as I walk into the room. "Hi," I say. "I'm tired. Can I join you?"

Whenever I do this, he willingly tries to shift his body to grant me space. Often it's not enough, so I roll the foot end of the bed away from the wall to give a little more room. Then I scrunch my body into whatever shape is available between him and the wall. It's something I've been doing a lot of lately. My body craves comfort and tucked under an extra blanket beside him I rest, read to him, or we listen to music. On this day I warn him that my hands are cold, but he laughs and lets me cuddle up to warm them against him, and that warms my heart.

When the tray comes for lunch, we eat together. He eats well and since I ordered a tray, too, I give him most of my dessert. He offers to share his jelly bread with me. I tell him I have my own and then offer mine to him. He eats half of it.

After lunch we talk. I want to address his worries but first I have to find out what they are. That's often a long process of listening to repeated sentence fragments and false starts. There are long silent spells while he tries to formulate his thoughts and words, then tries again.

I finally decipher that he is worried about money. Do you have enough? I addressed his fears telling him that the money he made teaching for twenty-one years is enough. It's the simplest explanation and satisfies him. Then something reminds him there is another worry— a lost check. It triggers my memory of his first year of teaching and how we misplaced one of his checks and the school had to issue a new one. The memory may have come back to haunt him. I tell him the checks are all accounted for. Now he seemed to relax.

I write with magic marker in big letters on a piece of notebook paper: "Our business is all taken care of and our checks are all accounted for." Then I pull out a notebook that I initially called his journal. I add this new page to the journal and read most of the journal to him, skipping pages that don't apply now. In the journal there are reminders for him. In large letters there are one or two short sentences to a page. "Dear Nelson, you are at Canterbury Villa. You live here. You are retired. You don't have to worry about anything. Your job is to enjoy your friends here. Someone comes to visit you every day. I'll see you soon. I miss you. Love, Ginnie." The aides know about the journal and sometimes use it to orient him or offer reassurances. Today he very slowly reads over the added page. He seemed satisfied but then asks, "Is food plentiful?" When I assure him it is, he pauses and then says, "—and the children?"

The children are lifelike baby dolls that are a part of the dementia unit. Nelson quickly attached to these babies. It is still an incredulous sight to see him interact with these dolls as if they are real. He gathers them in his room and covers them with blankets. He coos to them upon first seeing them when he comes back into the room or wakes up from a nap. "Hi, girls! Hey, how are you? Boy, you guys look good!" I assure him that the babies are getting enough to eat. The babies occasionally show evidence that Nelson has shared some food with them.

On this visit I suggest we sing to the babies. We place a baby on a chair facing us as we sit side by side on the bed. I hold another baby and begin to sing nursery songs. Nelson sings along, humming most of the time but getting a word in now and then when the lyrics are repetitious or simple. I sing, "Did you feed my cow?"

"Yes ma'am," he sings back.

"Could you tell me how?"

"Yes ma'am," he answers.

"What did you feed her?"

"Corn and hay." He remembers most of the answers in this song that we learned when I worked in a nursery school back in our first year of marriage. Then we sing, "Oh Mary Mack, Mack, Mack, all dressed in black, black, black." This one is also from our past and he joins in easily on the repetition.

Next we do finger plays with the babies. We do the first round of "Four little monkeys jumping on the bed." I move the arms of the baby on my lap as he watches. He makes voice inflections without words to follow along. "One fell off and she broke her head. Mamma called the doctor and the doctor said, 'No more monkeys jumping on the bed!'" For the next verse I pause at the very end and he comes in with a bit of sternness and without my help: "No more monkeys jumping on the bed!"

After some nursery songs and finger plays from memory I pull out another notebook. I had included the words to some favorite songs in large print in case he could follow along. There's a mixture of hymns, spirituals, camp songs, popular songs, and a child's song that reminds us of my father who learned it from his father. Today Nelson harmonizes, something we did more often in the earlier years of our marriage.

After some time he is ready to get up and walk. I ask if it's okay if I leave now and he indicates that it is. I read the journal to him one more time and then lay it down on his stand open to the new page. We walk together to the common area by the nurse's station. I wonder if he will try to follow me out, but he seems ready to shift his focus away from me, so we exchange a kiss and I walk to the door. He doesn't try to follow. I am relieved that for now at least he seems to have had his fears addressed.

An advantage to the location of this nursing home is the nature preserve that I pass on my way to and from the facility. Every day that I can, I stop here on my way home and walk one of the trails. I love these walks in the woods and feel a strong sense of Presence. My heart grows bigger, my body relaxes, and my spirit is renewed in the presence of the Creator and these trees that seem to wrap arms around me and tell me I'm going to be okay.

It is my sixty-seventh birthday, and I stop along one of the trails to sit briefly on a bench. I look up into a canopy of bare branches under a cluster of beech trees still holding stingily to their golden leaves. I sit listening to the sounds of quiet and wishing for some special woodland event to mark the day, but there is only stillness and one brown oak leaf doing its lazy circular downward dance in front of me. Maybe that will have to be my "something special" I think as I continue on my way. I am nearing the end of the trail when there is a loud, raucous call and I look up to see something flying toward me. It lodges in the underbrush nearby, and I am surprised to see a pheasant, something I've seen rarely, if at all, since my childhood days on a farm. I stay still, admiring its flamboyant, wide red neck ring, and listen as it calls back and forth to a similar voice in the distance. When their conversation lags, I walk on in thankfulness, knowing I've had something special to mark the mystery of Presence.

Lewy body has challenged my faith. I think, though, that I'm beginning to see that faith is not lack of questions, and love does not come without pain. I remember my friend Florrie's story. She was pushing her husband in his wheelchair when she encountered a couple of teenage girls. Their brief glance must have taken in something completely foreign to their young eyes and my friend thought but didn't say it: Take a good look girls. Yes, he's scruffy, drooling, slumped over, but this is what love looks like.

A new way of seeing love may be the gift of this relentless goodbye. I want to go forward knowing love and Presence even in the pain and loss. I hold on to hope that I will. In my most recent visit, we sat together eating lunch. I sneezed. I've begun saying the things out loud that he once might have said to me or that I need to hear. "Bless me," I said not glancing up. A touch to my forehead prompted me to look up. He had his arm outstretched, his fingers lightly touching me in a gesture of blessing. With that surprise, laughter bubbled from deep inside me. He smiled. I was blessed.

It is not an easy road, knowing where it leads but not fully knowing what lies ahead.

—Trudie Gauntt

What are the things in your life that might keep you from moving forward? What are the things that challenge your faith?

Afterword

Eric now lives in Arlington, Virginia, and is taking prerequisites for medical school. Amy teaches music in Newton, Kansas, and is taking a graduate educational leadership program. She lives with her husband, Joe Regier, and our grandchildren, Rich and Cora.

As for me, I continue to care for Nelson and work with my own health. Recently I learned that Benadrayl, the most effective medication I've found for treating my chemical sensitivities, may significantly increase the risk of dementia in the elderly. However, not taking it means even more isolation as I try to reduce the risk of reactions. I'm considering a move, but how can I be sure a dwelling I might choose will be safe for me?

This morning, when I turned off the nightlight at the top of the steps, I didn't bother to turn on the overhead light before descending a pitch-black stairway. I held the sturdy handrail thinking, I've done these steps a million times and I know what is there. I know the door at the bottom will open into the light.

Though my life often feels like that descent, I have to believe that there is light and healing and peace ahead. I know I will someday be able to see what I cannot always see now—that God has been here all along. That is the belief and hope. That is the rail I cling to.

Acknowledgments

Thank you above all to Nelson for suffering through this disease with unbelievable patience and good humor.

Thank you to our son, Eric Burkholder, and daughter, Amy Regier, for giving me reason to press on and for supporting my decisions and my writing.

To Cora June, our granddaughter, whose entrance into the world created many a smile on the faces of Papa Nelson and Grandma Gin and whose picture has been delightful company for Papa Nelson.

Thank you to my sister, Micki Horst, for generously sharing her expert knowledge of resources and consistently giving volumes of compassionate help and time, and to Roger Till for filling many a gap in repairs and maintenance around the house.

Thank you to our families, the Burkholders and the Horsts. Your numerous expressions of caring and support through this relentless goodbye have been invaluable.

Thank you to Bernie Hartman for standing with me in the first years of shock, anger, and fear and helping me get on with the task of grieving and mourning so that I could get on with the task of living and giving life a voice in my writing.

Thank you to Murray Mast for giving Nelson consistent and loving male companionship—and mowing our large lawn besides. You have given more than you know.

Thank you to Wendy Miller for reading my stories and helping me clarify and polish each one. You believed in my writing before I did and coached me into doing it better.

Thank you to Florrie Munat for reading each of my stories, giving me valuable feedback for the writing, and offering encouragement for the journey from a similar experience.

Thank you to Jane Yousey for listening to my verbal accounts, reading my written accounts, and never seeming to waver in validation and support when I got stuck in the mire of grief.

Thank you to Deb Miller for being an insightful friend and sharing this journey with me in so many ways through the years.

Thank you to all the people at First Mennonite Church for being a loving presence in Nelson's and my life journey.

Thank you to each person in the Inner Healing Sunday school class. Thank you for all the years that you sat with me through sometimes weekly acknowledgments of pain, listening to my fears, providing safe harbor, and sharing the healing journey.

Thank you to Angela Taylor who first invited me to post my writing on the Lewy body dementia (LBD) website where my book began to take form.

Thank you to caregivers across the country. You

have sent words of support for my caregiving and my writing. Your responses made writing rewarding and have shown me that I'm not alone in my struggle with this difficult disease.

Thank you to Julia Cameron for her book *The Artist's Way*. It was a significant link in the chain of people and events that brought me to publication. Thank you also to BOAS (Bettering Our Artist Selves) for going through Cameron's book with me not once but twice!

Thank you to Byron Rempel-Burkholder, my editor, who worked patiently with me in spite of my limited computer skills.

To all whom I've named and those whom I've forgotten who have reached out in any way, I want you to know you have made a difference. Life is better because of your prayers, the squeeze of your hand, the listening ear, the little expressions of love, and acts of kindness. You have kept me going, writing, and living with hope.

About the author

Ginnie H. Burkholder was born on her grandparents' homestead and grew up near Rittman, Ohio, where she was fifth in a family of eight children.

After their wedding, Ginnie and Nelson lived in Chicago where they served as volunteers at Bethel Mennonite Church. They both went on to graduate from the University of Illinois at Chicago Circle, each with a BA in elementary education. After graduating, they moved to Canton, Ohio, where they raised their son, Eric, and daughter, Amy.

Ginnie did substitute teaching and worked in a preschool during the years the children were in school. She and Nelson were both active at First Mennonite Church, serving over the years as elders, Sunday school teachers, singers in the choir, and worship leaders. Ginnie became involved with the American Friends Service Committee during the late seventies and was active with the Nuclear Weapons Freeze in peace-promoting activities.

Ginnie received an Elder Caregiver of the year award from the state of Ohio in 2007. She lives on the two acres she and Nelson have called home since 1986 and where sitting on the porch swing with friends is one of her favorite pastimes.